Trash to TREASURE

Recycling is no longer just a trend — it's a necessity for keeping our planet beautiful. You can do your part for the environment by making creative use of things you would ordinarily throw away! This enticing Trash to Treasure *volume features money-saving crafts ranging from furniture fix-ups to fun projects just for kids. We've included five sections, each packed full of fabulously crafty ideas. Check out Celebrations for birthday presents, holiday offerings, and even a gift for Grandparents' Day! Kids' Stuff includes items young ones will love, along with projects they can make. Green thumbs will find a fantastic collection of outdoor and indoor decor in Gardener's Treasures. Bargain enthusiasts won't be able to resist the ideas in our Flea Market Finds section, especially the new ways to jazz up tables, chairs, and more. And All Through the House will breathe new life into every room of your home with irresistible accents. Even if you've never picked up a glue gun, our detailed instructions and full-color photographs will walk you through each step to ensure success. With over 100 projects from which to choose, your only dilemma will be deciding which one to do first!*

Anne Childs

LEISURE ARTS, INC.
Little Rock, Arkansas

EDITORIAL STAFF

Vice President and Editor-in-Chief:
Anne Van Wagner Childs
Executive Director: Sandra Graham Case
Design Director: Patricia Wallenfang Sowers
Editorial Director: Susan Frantz Wiles
Publications Director: Kristine Anderson Mertes
Creative Art Director: Gloria Bearden

DESIGN
Senior Designers: Polly Tullis Browning, Sandra Spotts Ritchie, and Billie Steward
Designers: Diana Sanders Cates, Cherece Athy Cooper, Dani Martin, Anne Pulliam Stocks, and Linda Diehl Tiano
Executive Assistant: Debra Smith
Design Assistant: Melanie Vaughan

TECHNICAL
Managing Editor: Barbara McClintock Vechik
Senior Technical Writer: Jennifer Potts Hutchings
Technical Writers: Susan McManus Johnson and Theresa Hicks Young
Copy Editor: Susan Frazier
Production Assistant: Sharon Gillam

EDITORIAL
Managing Editor: Linda L. Trimble
Associate Editors: Darla Burdette Kelsay, Stacey Robertson Marshall, Taryn Stewart, and Hope Turner
Copy Editor: Terri Leming Davidson

ART
Book/Magazine Graphics Art Director: Diane Thoma
Senior Graphics Illustrator: Mark R. Potter
Graphics Illustrator: Linda Chambers
Color Technician: Mark Hawkins
Photography Stylists: Ellen J. Clifton, Sondra Daniel, Karen Hall, Tiffany Huffman, Aurora Huston, Elizabeth Lackey, and Janna Laughlin
Publishing Systems Administrator: Cindy Lumpkin
Publishing Systems Assistant: Myra Means

PROMOTIONS
Managing Editor: Alan Caudle
Associate Editor: Steven M. Cooper
Designer: Dale Rowett
Art Director: Linda Lovette Smart

BUSINESS STAFF

Publisher: Rick Barton
Vice President and General Manager: Thomas L. Carlisle
Vice President, Finance: Tom Siebenmorgen
Vice President, Retail Marketing: Bob Humphrey
Vice President, National Accounts: Pam Stebbins

Retail Marketing Director: Margaret Sweetin
General Merchandise Manager: Cathy Laird
Distribution Director: Rob Thieme
Retail Customer Service Manager: Wanda Price
Print Production Manager: Fred F. Pruss

Library of Congress Catalog Number 98-65089
International Standard Book Number 1-57486-152-2

10 9 8 7 6 5 4 3 2

TABLE OF CONTENTS

CRAFTY CELEBRATIONS 6

KIDS' STUFF 36

TABLE OF CONTENTS

GARDENER'S TREASURES..........54

FLEA MARKET FINDS.................78

TABLE OF CONTENTS

ALL THROUGH THE HOUSE 102

CRAFTY CELEBRATIONS

*U*nique creations make wonderful
decorative accessories for your home
and unforgettable surprises for
friends and family. To help
you turn common goods into
uncommon gifts and home accents,
we've collected an amazing
assortment of projects to craft
throughout the year. From Christmas
and birthdays to graduations and
"just because," this section is
brimming with creative ideas that
loved ones will cherish. You'll see
how old baskets become Easter
fancies, food cans and vinyl flooring
form a handsome desk set, and dryer
vent hoses produce a magical
pumpkin patch! The possibilities
are as endless as the smiles
they'll generate.

These candy-laden arrows are right on target for Valentine's Day. Fashioned from paper towel tubes and scraps of fabric, the love-struck offerings are perfect as party favors. Why not play Cupid and "aim" for the hearts of your friends and family!

PARTY FAVORS

Recycled items: paper towel tubes

For each favor, you will also need spray adhesive, 6" x 10" piece of fabric, tracing paper, poster board, gold acrylic paint, paintbrush, 15" of 1/8" dia. wooden dowel, gold spray-on glitter, hot glue gun, two 13" lengths of 1/4"w ecru ribbon, two 12" lengths of 1/8"w gold metallic ribbon, two 9" lengths of 1/8"w burgundy ribbon, wrapped candies to fill favor, 4" dia. gold paper doily, and assorted heart charms.

Allow paint and glitter spray to dry after each application.

1. Cut 6¹/₂" from one end of paper towel tube; discard remaining portion of tube. Apply spray adhesive to wrong side of fabric. With fabric extending 1³/₄" at each end, center and smooth fabric around tube.

2. Trace arrowhead and feather patterns, page 134, onto tracing paper; cut out. Using patterns, cut two arrowheads and one feather from poster board.

3. Paint arrowheads, both sides of feather, and wooden dowel. Apply glitter to arrowheads and feather.

4. Insert dowel through tube. Glue arrowheads together over one end of dowel and feather to opposite end.

5. Gathering fabric around one end of dowel, knot one length of each ribbon around gathers. Fill favor with candy.

6. Gathering fabric around opposite end of dowel, knot remaining ribbons around gathers.

7. Apply spray adhesive to wrong side of doily; smooth around favor. Tie charms to ends of burgundy ribbons.

DECOUPAGED CIGAR BOX

*P*erfect *for storing old love letters and valentines, this romantic notion box once held cigars! A coat of spray paint, a lacy paper doily, and motifs clipped from wrapping paper turn a masculine box into a sentimental keepsake she'll adore.*

Recycled item: cigar box

You will also need white spray primer, pink spray paint, wood-tone spray, craft glue, foam brush, paper doily to fit on lid of cigar box, Victorian-motif wrapping paper, 17" of 1¹/₂"w red wired ribbon, hot glue gun, 24" of white string pearls, and items to decorate box (we used charms, buttons, and a ribbon flower).

Allow primer, paint, and wood-tone spray to dry after each application.

1. Spray box with primer, then paint. Lightly apply wood-tone spray to box.
2. Mix one part craft glue with one part water. Use foam brush to apply glue mixture to back of doily. Position doily on lid of box; smooth in place and allow to dry.
3. Cut desired motifs from paper. Use foam brush to apply glue mixture to back of motifs. Arrange motifs on box lid; smooth in place and allow to dry. Apply glue mixture over entire box lid; allow to dry.
4. Tie ribbon into a bow. Hot glue bow, pearls, and decorative items to box as desired.
5. Lightly apply wood-tone spray to box.

PORTRAIT VASE

*L*ooking *for a special Mother's Day gift? Decorate a ho-hum vase with family photographs and fill it with a bouquet of her favorite flowers! Painted "frames" showcase photocopied snapshots.*

PHOTO VASE

Recycled item: vase

You will also need gold and black Delta CeramDecor™ Air-Dry Perm Enamel™ paint, paintbrushes, color photocopy of desired photograph(s), craft glue, and a foam brush.

Allow paint to dry after each application.

1. For each photocopy, applying three coats of paint, paint a 1³/₄" x 2¹/₄" black rectangle on vase.
2. For "frame," paint a ³/₈"w gold border around black rectangle. Add black details and "hanger" to frame.
3. Cut out desired portion of photocopy to fit inside frame. Mix one part glue with one part water. Use foam brush to apply glue mixture to wrong side of photocopy. Position photocopy in frame; smooth in place. Allowing to dry between coats, lightly apply several coats of glue mixture over photocopy.

SPRING ABLOOM

*Y*ou'll want to display *this lovely Easter egg ornament all spring. A painted foam egg blooms with soft color when adorned with silk flowers and decoupaged motifs. Satin cord frames the wistful images.*

EASTER EGG ORNAMENT

Recycled items: artificial floral stems

You will also need dark purple acrylic paint, paintbrush, 3³/₈" x 4⁷/₈" plastic foam egg, Easter-motif wrapping paper, craft glue, foam brush, decorative satin cord, glass seed beads, and straight pins.

1. Paint egg; allow to dry.
2. Cut four motifs no larger than 1¹/₂" x 1³/₄" from wrapping paper. Mix one part glue with one part water. Use foam brush to apply glue mixture to back of motifs. Spacing motifs evenly around egg, smooth motifs in place. Apply glue mixture over motifs; allow to dry.
3. Cut four 25" lengths from cord. Glue one cord length around each motif.
4. Remove flowers from stems. For each flower, thread two beads and one flower head onto one straight pin. Overlapping as necessary to cover egg, insert pins into egg.

5. Cut one 5" length and one 9" length from cord. For hanger, fold 5" length of cord in half; use pins to attach ends to top of egg. Tie 9" length of cord into a bow; pin bow to top of egg.

PAINTED WHIMSY

*T*his whimsical yet durable
Easter floorcloth is created by
painting the back of a leftover
piece of vinyl flooring.

EASTER FLOOR MAT

Recycled item: 22" x 30" piece of vinyl
flooring

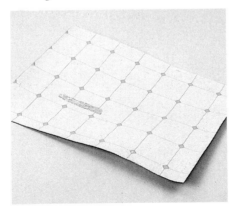

You will also need white, yellow, pink,
purple, blue, blue green, and green
acrylic paint; paintbrushes; yardstick;
pencil; stencil plastic; craft knife; cutting
mat; stencil brushes; and clear acrylic
spray sealer.

*Refer to Painting Techniques, page 156,
before beginning project. Allow paint
and sealer to dry after each application.*

1. For floor mat, base coat back of
vinyl flooring piece with two coats of
white paint.
2. Use yardstick and pencil to lightly draw
thirty-two 2" squares at center of mat for
checkerboard, a 1"w inner border around
checkerboard, and a 1"w outer border
around edge of mat.
3. Paint alternate checkerboard squares
pink, inner border green, and outer
border purple.
4. Using egg pattern, page 152, follow
Stenciling, page 157, to stencil eggs onto
mat. Paint desired designs on eggs.
5. Apply two to three coats of sealer
to mat.

Make a lovely impression with gifts delivered in these charming Easter baskets. Floral motifs and dimensional roses are easily fashioned from wrapping paper. Pastel paint and pretty odds-and-ends add to the beauty of these springtime totes.

EASTER BASKETS

PAPER ROSES

Recycled item: floral-motif wrapping paper
You will also need a hot glue gun and tracing paper.

1. Cut four 3" x 13" strips from wrapping paper.
2. For each small rose, fold one end of one strip 1/4" to wrong side. Matching wrong sides and long edges, fold strip in half. With long folded edge at top and beginning with unfolded end, roll one-fourth of strip tightly to form rose center; glue to secure. Wrap remainder of strip loosely around center, folding small uneven pleats along bottom edge; glue bottom edge to secure.
3. For large rose, trace petal pattern, page 147, onto tracing paper; cut out. Using pattern, cut six petals from remaining wrapping paper. Curl side edges of each petal around a pencil (Fig. 1).

Fig. 1

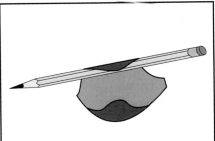

4. Glue petals around one small rose.

PAPER CUTOUTS

Recycled items: floral-motif wrapping paper and poster board
You will also need craft glue.

Glue portion of wrapping paper with desired motifs onto poster board; allow to dry. Cut out motifs.

BASKETS

Recycled items: baskets (we used one basket with a handle and one basket with a lid) and floral-motif wrapping paper
You will also need pink spray paint, paintbrush, white acrylic paint, hot glue gun, Paper Roses, Paper Cutouts, and additional items to decorate baskets (we used satin ribbon, sheer ribbon, a button, and a 5" dia. crocheted doily).

Allow paint to dry after each application.

1. For each basket, spray paint basket pink. Use a dry paintbrush to lightly paint basket white.
2. Arrange and glue roses, cutouts, and decorative items to basket as desired.
3. For basket filler, cut wrapping paper into 1/4" strips. Fill basket with strips.

Our handy "brag box" fits easily into a purse, so it's a great "any occasion" gift for the grandma on the go. She'll love keeping photos of smiling loved ones in the wrapping paper-embellished tin.

Recycled items: small tin box with lid and floral-motif wrapping paper

You will also need white spray primer, acrylic paint to coordinate with wrapping paper, paintbrush, spray adhesive, craft knife, hot glue gun, $1/8$" dia. acrylic jewels, $1/8$"w ribbon, black permanent medium-point marker, card stock, gallon-size clear food storage plastic bag, and desired photographs.

Allow primer and paint to dry after each application.

1. Apply primer to inside and outside of box.
2. Use acrylic paint to paint inside and outside of bottom of box.
3. Leaving at least $3/4$" between shapes, draw around lid on wrong side of wrapping paper twice. For inside of lid, cut out one paper piece inside drawn line.

Apply spray adhesive to wrong side of paper piece. Smooth paper piece to inside of lid. For outside of lid, cut out remaining paper piece $3/8$" outside drawn line. Apply spray adhesive to wrong side of paper piece. Position and smooth paper piece onto top and sides of lid. Use craft knife to trim edges of paper even with edge of lid. Glue jewels to lid as desired.

4. Measure around lid; add $1/4$". Cut a length of ribbon the determined measurement. Overlapping ends at back, glue ribbon around lid.
5. Use marker to write "Grandma's Brag Box" inside lid.
6. For photograph holder, measure width of box; subtract $1/2$", then multiply by 5. Measure length of box; subtract $1/4$". Cut a piece of card stock the determined measurements. Divide card stock into five equal sections. Use a pencil to lightly mark sections.
7. Insert card stock in corner of bag. Using a short stitch length, sew along end opposite corner and along each drawn line. Cutting holder close to stitching along outer edges, cut holder from bag. Fold holder accordion-style along stitched lines.
8. Trim photographs to fit in holders. Place photographs in holder. Glue one end of photograph holder to front inside edge of box.

BEADED FANCIES

*F*un and easy to do, these colorful eyeglass holders are great birthday gifts for teens. The colorful cords, made by stringing beads saved from broken necklaces, will be a hit at the beach — or anywhere!

BEADED EYEGLASS HOLDERS

Recycled items: ⅛"w rubber bands and beads from broken necklaces

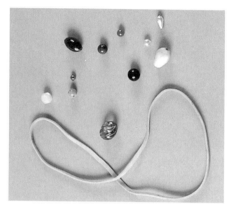

You will also need a sharp needle that will fit through beads, 34" of heavy-duty thread, and craft glue.

1. Cut two 1" lengths from rubber band.
2. For each eyeglass holder, matching short ends, fold one rubber band piece in half. Using needle and thread, insert needle through ends of rubber band piece. Thread beads onto thread. Matching short ends, fold remaining rubber band piece in half. Insert needle through ends of rubber band piece. Knot thread ends to secure. Apply glue to knots; allow to dry.

FRAMED FOR HIM

*N*eed *a birthday gift for him that says "You're special"? Give a facelift to a timeworn photo frame! It's easy to create the classic look of tortoiseshell using gold paint and several shades of wood stain.*

TORTOISESHELL FRAME

Recycled item: wooden frame

You will also need newspaper; gold spray paint; paintbrushes; Minwax® Polyshades® oak, walnut, and mahogany gloss wood stains with varnish; and turpentine.

Allow paint and turpentine to dry after each application. Use a clean paintbrush for each stain and turpentine.

1. Cover work area with newspaper.
2. Spray paint frame.
3. Allowing stain to drip from paintbrush, drop small drops of one stain randomly onto frame; do not stroke with paintbrush. While stain is still wet, drop small drops of turpentine over stain. Repeat with remaining stains to cover frame.

Dad will be impressed when you give him this attractive desk set for Father's Day. And he'll never guess that it's fashioned from recycled food cans and a piece of vinyl flooring!

MEN'S DESK SET

Recycled items: 17" x 22" piece of cardboard, 17" x 22" piece of vinyl flooring, three food cans, and a belt buckle to accommodate 5/8"w ribbon

You will also need a hot glue gun, ecru spray paint, 5/8"w and 1¹/₂"w grosgrain ribbon, fabric, batting, pinking shears, and ecru felt.

BLOTTER
1. Glue cardboard piece to right side of vinyl. For right side of blotter, spray paint wrong side of vinyl; allow to dry.
2. Glue a 22" length of 1¹/₂"w ribbon along top and bottom of blotter.
3. For each side of blotter, cut one 8" x 19" piece from fabric and one 3" x 17" piece from batting. Matching wrong sides and long edges, press fabric piece in half. Centering batting top to bottom, insert batting in fold of fabric. Glue edges together. Position fabric pieces on blotter with glued edges extending 1" beyond blotter. Glue short ends, then remaining edges of fabric pieces to back of blotter.
4. Center a 19" length of 5/8"w ribbon along each fabric-covered end of blotter; glue ends to back.

DESK ORGANIZER
1. For each can, measure height of can between rims. Measure circumference of can. Cut a piece of batting the determined measurements. Glue batting around can.
2. Measure height of can between rims. Measure circumference of can; add ¹/₂". Cut a piece from fabric the determined measurements. Overlapping fabric at back, glue fabric around can.
3. Using circumference measurement determined in Step 2 and pinking shears, cut two bias fabric strips 1"w by the determined measurement. Overlapping fabric strips at back and with strips extending ¹/₂" beyond rims, glue strips around top and bottom rims of can. Fold top strip to inside of can; glue to secure. Fold bottom strip to bottom of can; glue to secure.
4. Draw around bottom of can on felt. Cutting inside drawn line, cut out circle. Glue circle to inside bottom of can (trimming if necessary). Measure inside height of can. Measure inside circumference of can. Cut a piece of felt the determined measurements. Use pinking shears to trim ¹/₈" from one long edge. With pinked edge at top, glue felt to inside of can.
5. For can with buckle, measure circumference of can; add 3". Cut a length of 5/8"w ribbon the determined measurement. Glue one end of ribbon around center of buckle. Wrap ribbon around can. Thread remaining ribbon end through buckle; glue to secure. Trimming to fit, glue ribbon around remaining cans.
6. Glue cans together to form organizer.

Have a fabulous Fourth of July with this patriotic banner! Using a little creativity and items like an old oxford shirt, a paper bag, and cardboard tubes, you can make an eye-catching decoration in no time.

PATRIOTIC BANNER

Recycled items: large brown paper bag, adult-size oxford shirt to coordinate with theme, four toilet paper tubes, and one 1¹/₄" dia. wrapping paper tube

You will also need paper-backed fusible web, decorative-edge craft scissors, tracing paper, yellow card stock, red and blue colored pencils, spray adhesive, red-and-white stripe fabric, navy print fabric, hot glue gun, white cord, and a star-shaped craft punch.

1. Cut bag open along one fold. Cut away bottom. Press with a warm, dry iron.
2. Cut one 14" x 19³/₄" piece for backing and three 1" x 14" strips for hanging loops from bag. Cut one 12" x 19³/₄" piece each from oxford shirt and paper-backed fusible web.
3. For banner, fuse web to wrong side of shirt piece. Center shirt piece web side down on backing piece; fuse in place. Use craft scissors to trim short ends (top and bottom) of banner.
4. Trace small and large star patterns, page 142, onto tracing paper; cut out. Using patterns, cut three small stars and one large star from card stock. Use colored pencils to write "Happy 4th of July" and add details to stars. Apply spray adhesive to wrong side of stars. Arrange and smooth stars onto banner.

5. For each firecracker, cutting from end to end, cut a ¹/₂"w strip from toilet paper tube; discard ¹/₂"w strip. Apply spray adhesive to wrong sides of a 5¹/₂" square of stripe fabric and a 2" x 5¹/₂" piece of print fabric. Center and smooth stripe fabric around firecracker. With print fabric extending ¹/₂" at one end of firecracker, smooth fabric around one end of firecracker. Clipping as necessary, fold and smooth ends of fabrics to inside of firecracker.
6. Matching cut edges at back, glue firecrackers to banner.
7. For each fuse, glue 1" of a 3" length of cord inside firecracker; glue remaining portion of fuse to banner.
8. Use colored pencils to add details to sides of banner and each hanging loop. Use craft punch to punch stars from card stock. Glue stars to banner and hanging loops.
9. Glue 2" of each 1" x 14" hanging loop together. Spacing evenly across top of banner, glue ends of hanging loops to back of banner.
10. For hanger, cut a 14" length from wrapping paper tube. Apply spray adhesive to wrong sides of a 4¹/₂" x 15" piece of stripe fabric and two 2" x 4¹/₂" pieces of print fabric. Center and smooth stripe fabric around hanger. For each end, with one print fabric piece extending ¹/₂" past end, smooth fabric around hanger. Clipping as necessary, fold and press ends of fabrics to inside of hanger. Glue 1" of a 3" length of cord to inside of each end of hanger. Place hanger through hanging loops.

CLASSY CUBE

Your children won't sweat the cost of a Grandparents' Day gift when they use the "good" sides of their broken compact disc cases to create this classy photo cube. Display favorite baby pictures, or fill the cube with current snapshots. Grandparents' Day is celebrated on the first Sunday in September following Labor Day.

CD CASE PHOTO CUBE

Recycled items: five compact disc cases

You will also need household cement, lightweight corrugated cardboard, transparent tape, five photographs, and 33" of decorative satin cord.

Allow household cement to dry after each application.

1. Separate top from each case. Carefully break off any extending tabs.
2. Glue four tops together to form sides of cube. Glue remaining top over sides of cube.
3. Cut five 4⅞" x 5⅛" pieces from corrugated cardboard. Cut a 4" square opening in center of each cardboard piece. Aligning edges, glue one cardboard piece to each side and top of cube.

4. Trimming to fit and centering image in cardboard opening, tape photographs to inside of cube. Tie cord into a bow around top of cube; spot glue to secure. Knot ends of cord.

JUST FOR HER

A simple coffee creamer canister lies beneath the tropical exterior of our seashore-inspired container. For a soothing birthday gift, fill the canister with her favorite scented bath salts.

BATH SALTS CONTAINER

Recycled item: coffee creamer container with hinged lid

You will also need beige and gold acrylic paint, paintbrush, natural sponge, batting, hot glue gun, fabric, ¼"w gimp trim, 27" of 1⅞"w wired ribbon, and seashells.

Refer to Painting Techniques, page 156, before beginning project. Allow paint to dry after each application.

1. Paint top of container beige. Sponge paint top of container gold.
2. Cut a piece of batting to fit around container. Wrap batting around container; glue to secure. Trimming to fit and overlapping ends at back, wrap fabric around container; glue to secure.
3. Trimming to fit, glue trim around top and bottom edges of container.
4. Tie ribbon into a bow around container. Glue one seashell to opening tab and remaining seashells to knot of bow.

PUMPKIN PATCH

*Y*ou don't have to make a trip to the pumpkin patch to create this charming tabletop display! Orange and green paint turn a recycled dryer vent hose and large twigs into perfect pumpkins.

DRYER VENT HOSE PUMPKINS

Recycled items: dryer vent hose and large twigs

For each pumpkin, you will also need a hot glue gun, garden clippers, orange and green spray paint, 18" of medium-gauge craft wire, and 12" of 1¹/₂"w green wired ribbon.

Allow paint to dry after each application.

1. For pumpkin, with hose extended, cut a 20" to 25" length from hose. Matching open ends, form hose into a circle; glue to secure.
2. For stem, use garden clippers to cut 6" from twig.
3. Spray paint pumpkin orange. Lightly spray top of pumpkin and stem green.
4. Apply glue to one end of stem. Insert stem in opening at center of pumpkin. Curl 16" of one end of wire around a pencil; remove pencil. Wrap opposite end of wire around stem.
5. For leaves, knot ribbon around stem.

PERKY PUMPKIN PACKAGE

reat a favorite ghoul or goblin to a crafty container filled with Halloween goodies! Bases cut from two-liter bottles form the grinning jack-o'-lantern, and the leaves are made from a brown paper bag. Clip a twig from your backyard to give it a stem.

PUMPKIN TREAT HOLDER

Recycled items: two 2-liter plastic soda bottles, brown paper bag, and a twig

You will also need a craft knife; orange spray paint; craft glue; green, brown, and black acrylic paint; paintbrushes; tracing paper; three 2" lengths of floral wire; garden clippers; and household cement.

Allow paint, craft glue, and household cement to dry after each application. Use craft glue for all gluing unless otherwise indicated.

1. Measuring 2¹/₂" from bottom of bottle, draw a line around each bottle. Use craft knife to cut away top sections of bottles along drawn line. Cut a 1¹/₄"w ring from top section of one bottle. Cut across ring to make strip. Discard remaining top sections.

2. Spray paint outside of bottle bottoms and both sides of strip orange.
3. For bottom of treat holder, overlapping ends as necessary and with ⁵/₈" extending above cut edge, glue strip around inside of one section. For top of treat holder, place remaining section over bottom of treat holder.
4. Paint eyes and nose on top half and mouth on bottom half of treat holder.

5. Trace leaf pattern, page 153, onto tracing paper; cut out. Using pattern, cut six leaves from brown paper bag. Paint leaves green. Paint brown veins on leaves.
6. For each leaf, leaving ⁵/₈" to 1" of wire extending from base of leaf, glue two leaves together over one length of wire. Shape wire as desired.
7. For stem, use garden clippers to cut a 1¹/₄" long twig. Use household cement to glue wire ends of leaves, then stem to top of treat holder.

EAT MORE PORK!

A *turkey's attempt to survive the Thanksgiving season is the inspiration behind this lighthearted accent. Decorate the wreath with adorable turkeys crafted from flattened aluminum cans, metal bottle caps, and twigs to add holiday spirit to a window.*

Recycled items: 12-oz. aluminum beverage cans, twigs, and metal bottle caps for heads

You will also need utility scissors; hot glue gun; craft knife; white spray primer; glossy wood-tone spray; yellow and black acrylic paint; paintbrushes; tracing paper; white, yellow, and red craft foam; 1/8" dia. and 1/16" dia. hole punches; decorative-edge craft scissors; white card stock; black permanent medium-point marker; 6" of jute twine; 14" dia. straw wreath; 3 yds. of wired ribbon; artificial acorn spray; wire cutters; and floral wire.

Allow primer, wood-tone spray, and paint to dry after each application.

1. For each turkey body, step on one can to flatten can.

2. Use utility scissors to cut through opening of one unflattened beverage can; cut away and discard top of can. Trim can to within 2" from bottom of can. Cut can in half lengthwise (Fig. 1).

Fig. 1

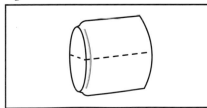

3. For feathers, cutting to within 1/4" of bottom of can, cut down sides of each can half at 1/2" intervals. Flatten each can half with feathers extending outward. Trim corners from each feather. Arranging feathers, glue can halves together. Glue feathers to back of body.

4. For neck, cut a 2 1/2" long twig. Use craft knife to make a pilot hole at top of body. Apply glue to one end of neck; insert in hole. Glue head to opposite end.

5. Apply primer, then wood-tone spray to body, feathers, neck, and head. Paint accents on feathers.

6. Trace beak, wattle, and feet patterns, page 147, onto tracing paper; cut out. Using patterns, cut beak from yellow craft foam, wattle from red craft foam, and feet from white craft foam. Use 1/8" dia. hole punch to punch eyes from white craft foam.

7. Arrange and glue eyes, beak, and wattle on head. Use black paint to add pupils to eyes.

8. For each leg, cut a 2 1/2" long twig. Glue feet to one end of each leg. Paint legs and feet yellow. Use craft knife to make a pilot hole for each leg at bottom of body. Apply glue to end of each leg; insert legs in holes.

9. For sign, use craft scissors to cut a 1 1/2" x 2" piece of card stock. Use marker to write "EAT MORE PORK" on sign. Use 1/16" dia. hole punch to punch one hole in each top corner of sign. Knotting ends at front, insert ends of twine through holes. Place sign around turkey's neck.

10. For wreath, wrap two yards of ribbon around wreath. Tie remaining ribbon into a bow. Glue bow and acorn spray to top of wreath. Use wire to attach turkeys to wreath.

WHIMSICAL REINDEER

*A*dd a touch of whimsy to
your holiday with this playful
reindeer, crafted from a small
milk carton. His wacky look is
completed with twig antlers,
raffia hair, wiggle eyes, and
a glass ornament nose.

MILK CARTON REINDEER

Recycled items: pint-size milk carton
and twigs

You will also need a hot glue gun, white
spray primer, wood-tone spray, craft
knife, 1¼" dia. red glass ball ornament,
14mm wiggle eyes, black permanent
medium-point marker, natural raffia,
push pin, miniature artificial redbird, and
8" of ⅝"w ribbon.

1. For reindeer, use glue to reseal carton.
Allowing to dry between coats, apply
primer, then wood-tone spray to carton.
2. For nose, use craft knife to cut a small
"X" in center front of carton slightly
smaller than diameter of ornament cap.
Remove cap and wire from ornament.
Apply glue around top of ornament.
Carefully insert top of ornament into hole.
3. Glue eyes to carton and use marker to
draw mouth and eyebrows. Glue several

lengths of raffia to top of carton for hair.
Trim ends of raffia; spot glue to secure.
4. For antlers, use push pin to make one
pilot hole in each side of top of carton.

Apply glue to one end of each twig; insert
twigs in holes. Glue redbird to one antler.
5. For bow tie, tie ribbon into a bow. Glue
bow tie to reindeer.

SANTA'S EXPRESS

*T*ucked inside this special-delivery container, a child's wish list is sure to get Santa's attention! Just cover a paper towel tube with festive fabric, affix the photocopied paper "mailing label," and cap the ends with muffin cups and ribbon.

"LETTER TO SANTA" HOLDER

Recycled item: paper towel tube

You will also need spray adhesive, 6" x 13" piece of fabric, colored pencils, photocopy of label (page 135), letter to Santa, two 1³/₄" dia. white baking cup liners, and two 15¹/₂" lengths of ¹/₈"w green grosgrain ribbon.

1. Apply spray adhesive to wrong side of fabric. With fabric extending 1" at each end of tube, center and smooth fabric around tube. Clipping as necessary, fold and press ends to inside of tube.
2. Use colored pencils to color label; cut out. Apply spray adhesive to wrong side of label. Center and smooth label onto tube.
3. Roll and insert letter into tube. Place one liner over each end of tube. Tie one ribbon length into a bow around each liner.

ELEGANT PATCHES

Painted in shimmering tones, this elegant tree trimmer is created from a foam ball, brown paper scraps, and a mesh produce bag.

TORN BAG ORNAMENT

Recycled items: brown paper bag, mesh produce bag, and a plastic bottle cap

You will also need silver, gold, and copper acrylic paint; paintbrushes; craft glue; foam brush; 4" dia. plastic foam ball; gold spray paint; hot glue gun; and 7¹/₂" of gold cord.

1. Cut three 3" x 5" shapes from paper bag. Painting each shape a different color, paint shapes silver, gold, and copper; allow to dry. Tear shapes into 1" to 2" pieces.

2. Mix one part craft glue with one part water. Use foam brush to apply glue mixture to back of paper bag pieces. For ornament, overlapping pieces as necessary to cover foam ball, position and smooth paper bag pieces on foam ball; allow to dry. Apply glue mixture over ornament; allow to dry.

3. Cut a 5¹/₂" x 14¹/₂" piece from produce bag. Spray paint cap and produce bag piece gold; allow to dry.

4. For top of ornament, hot glue cap to ball. Hot glue ends of cord to center of cap.

5. Tie produce bag piece into a bow. Hot glue bow to cap, covering cord ends.

NOT EVEN A MOUSE

*N*o one will ever guess that this adorable trio was created from empty wine bottles! Paint and varnish each container, then glue on foam-ball noses and craft-foam ears and mittens. Give them tiny "songbooks," and you'll have a fun Yuletide accent.

WINE BOTTLE CAROLERS

Recycled items: three wine bottles

You will also need white spray primer; white, pink, tan, and black acrylic paint; paintbrushes; tracing paper; transfer paper; satin varnish; green card stock; photocopy of sheet music; craft glue; red and black craft foam; low-temperature glue gun; and three 2" dia. plastic foam balls.

Allow primer, paint, varnish, and glue to dry after each application.

1. For each caroler, apply primer to bottle. Paint bottle tan.
2. For mouth, trace pattern, page 154, onto tracing paper. Use transfer paper to transfer mouth to caroler. Paint mouth black and teeth white.
3. Apply varnish to caroler.

4. For songbook, cut one 3½" x 6" piece each from card stock and photocopy. Use craft glue to glue photocopy to card stock. Matching short ends, fold songbook in half.
5. Trace ear and mitten patterns, page 154, onto tracing paper; cut out. Using patterns, cut ears from black craft foam and mittens from red craft foam.

Use dry paintbrush and pink paint to add ear details.
6. Hot glue wrist areas of mittens to caroler and songbook to mittens. Hot glue ears to caroler.
7. For nose, paint rim of bottle and plastic foam ball black. Hot glue nose to top of bottle.

REACH FOR THE STARS

*R*each *for the stars with this quick-to-assemble decoration! Cut from foam food trays, the celestial trio is painted, embellished with acrylic jewels, and strung from a silver ribbon.*

FOAM TRAY HANGING STARS

Recycled items: foam food trays

You will also need tracing paper, craft knife, cutting mat, Design Master® silver spray paint, low-temperature glue gun, assorted acrylic jewels, and 26" of ¼"w silver ribbon.

1. Trace small, medium, and large star patterns, page 134, onto tracing paper; cut out. Using patterns and craft knife, cut two of each star from trays.
2. Spray paint stars; allow to dry.
3. Glue acrylic jewels to one side of each star.
4. For hanger, make a 4" loop at one end of ribbon; glue end to secure. With ribbon between stars, glue small, medium, then large stars together.

RINGING IN THE YEAR

*R*ing in the new year with a festive toast — and display your holiday "spirits" on this decorative wine bottle coaster. The base is made of corks tied with raffia. A clay saucer covered in beverage bottle labels rests on top to hold a bottle of wine. You can use the coaster all year long!

CORK COASTER

Recycled items: beverage bottle labels and thirty-nine 1³/₄"h straight-sided bottle corks

You will also need a 5" dia. clay saucer, craft glue, foam brush, hot glue gun, wire cutters, medium-gauge craft wire, wood-tone spray, and natural raffia.

1. For saucer, mix one part craft glue with one part water. Use foam brush to apply glue mixture to backs of labels. Arrange labels on saucer; smooth in place. Apply glue mixture over labels; allow to dry.

2. For coaster, hot glue six corks around one cork to form inner ring; wrap wire around ring. Repeat to hot glue and wire thirteen corks for center ring, then nineteen corks for outer ring.

3. Lightly apply wood-tone spray to saucer and cork ring; allow to dry.

4. Tie several lengths of raffia into a bow around coaster to cover wire. Place saucer on coaster.

KIDS' STUFF

*W*hat better way to encourage creativity in kids than with crafty projects! We've gathered an exciting collection that includes wonderful things you can make for your children, as well as lots of stuff they can make themselves! Using items that would otherwise be thrown away, you can show kids how to recycle ordinary discards into toys, accessories, and gifts. Transform an egg carton into a dainty jewelry box, or make a checker game from denim scraps and plastic bottle caps. There are also ideas just for teens — T-shirts become comfy pillows in minutes, and old blue jeans become a trendy locker organizer. So let the youngsters in on the fun, and craft to your hearts' delight!

NIGHTSTAND STOVE

Cook up a creative play center when you transform a battered nightstand into this cute "stove." Kids will spend hours making up their own recipes for fun, and at the end of the day, they can put their toys away in the drawers!

Recycled item: nightstand

You will also need items listed under *Preparing an Item for Painting* (page 156), handsaw, 3"w baseboard, 1" x 6" pine board, wood glue, white spray primer, tracing paper, transfer paper, black and assorted colors of acrylic paint, paintbrushes, liner brush, permanent medium-point marker, platinum spray paint, four 1¹⁄₂" dia. wooden wheels, four ¹⁄₂" dia. wooden cap buttons, craft drill, 1"l wood screws, 2"w stencil with repeat, stencil brush, and matte acrylic spray sealer.

Allow primer, paint, glue, and sealer to dry after each application.

1. Remove handles from nightstand. Follow *Preparing an Item for Painting*, page 156, to prepare nightstand.

2. Measure width of nightstand. Use handsaw to cut one length each from baseboard and pine board the determined measurement. Glue baseboard to one edge of pine board.

3. Apply two to three coats primer to nightstand, baseboard, and pine board.

4. For clock, trace Heart A pattern, page 137, onto tracing paper. Use transfer paper to transfer design to baseboard. Paint heart. Use liner brush to outline heart in a contrasting color. Use marker to draw clockface on heart.

5. Spray paint handles and wheels platinum. Paint cap buttons black. For knobs on stove, use drill and wood screws to loosely attach wheels to baseboard. Glue cap buttons to heads of screws. For stove settings, paint one black line on each wheel and continue onto baseboard.

6. With baseboard resting on top of nightstand, use drill and wood screws to attach pine board to back of nightstand.

7. Paint a 2¹⁄₂"w border in a contrasting color at top and near bottom of nightstand. Using stencil, follow Step 3 of *Stenciling*, page 157, to stencil design in desired color along borders.

8. Trace Heart B and burner patterns, page 137, onto tracing paper. Use transfer paper to transfer four hearts randomly to each side of stove and three burners to top of stove. Using assorted colors, paint each heart. Use liner brush to outline each heart in a contrasting color. Paint designs on hearts as desired. Paint burners black.

9. Replace handles on stove. Apply two to three coats of sealer to stove.

THIS LITTLE PIGGY

*S*aving money has never been this much fun! A little girl will love dropping her precious pennies into this perky piggy bank. Easy to make from a salt container, bottle cap, and corks, our posy-bedecked pig makes a perfect project for kids.

POSY PIGGY BANK

Recycled items: salt container, plastic bottle cap, and four bottle corks

You will also need a craft knife, pink and black spray paint, photocopy of eyes and flowers (page 144), craft glue, foam brush, black permanent fine-point marker, hot glue gun, tracing paper, pink craft foam, and a black chenille stem.

Use hot glue for all gluing unless otherwise indicated.

1. For bank, remove wrapper from salt container. For coin slot, use craft knife to cut a $1/4$" x 1" slit in one side of container.
2. Spray paint bank and bottle cap pink and corks black; allow to dry.
3. Cut eyes from photocopy. Mix one part craft glue with one part water. Use foam brush to apply glue mixture to wrong side of each eye. Position and smooth eyes onto one end of bank; allow to dry.

4. Cut flowers from photocopy. Use foam brush to apply glue mixture to wrong side of flowers. Arrange flowers on bank; smooth in place. Apply glue mixture over entire bank; allow to dry.
5. For snout, use marker to draw nose and mouth on bottle cap. Glue snout to bank.

6. Trace ear patterns, page 144, onto tracing paper; cut out. Using patterns, cut ears from craft foam. Matching centers of tabs to shape ears, glue ears to bank.
7. For legs, trimming as necessary with craft knife, glue corks to bottom of bank.
8. For tail, cut a $9^1/2$" length from chenille stem. Wrap length around a pencil; remove pencil. Glue tail to bank.

40

A CHILD'S COOKERY

*D*on't waste money on expensive kitchen toys when you can make these charming canisters and pans from empty cardboard and plastic containers. In no time your child's "kitchen" will be overflowing with creativity!

CANISTERS AND PANS

Recycled items: five assorted containers with lids

You will also need white spray primer, craft knife, cutting mat, assorted colors of acrylic paint, paintbrushes, foam core board, tracing paper, transfer paper, liner brush, assorted wooden knobs, hot glue gun, utility scissors, two jumbo craft sticks, and masking tape.

Allow primer and paint to dry after each application.

1. Apply primer to outsides of containers and lids.
2. For pans, use craft knife to cut 1¹/₂" to 2¹/₂" from bottoms of two containers. Paint pans.
3. For each pan lid, draw around bottom of pan on foam core board. Use craft knife to cut out circle ¹/₄" outside drawn

line. Trace Heart A pattern, page 152, onto tracing paper. Use transfer paper to transfer desired number of hearts to top of each lid. Using assorted colors, paint each heart. Use liner brush to outline each heart in a contrasting color. Paint designs on hearts as desired. Paint knob. Center and glue knob on lid.
4. For pan with handle, use utility scissors to cut craft sticks in half. Matching cut ends, stack halves and use masking tape to tape together. Paint handle. Use craft knife to cut slit large enough to insert

handle in side of pan. Apply glue to cut end of handle and insert in slit.
5. For each canister, trace Heart A or Heart B pattern, page 152, onto tracing paper. Use transfer paper to transfer hearts to sides of remaining containers. Using assorted colors, paint each heart. Use liner brush to outline each heart in a contrasting color. Paint designs on hearts as desired.
6. For each canister lid, paint lid of container and knob. Add highlight to knob. Center and glue knob on lid.

41

SOCKS THE CAT

Fashioned from an orphaned tube sock, this adorable feline is reminiscent of the homemade dolls of yesteryear. His face is created with felt appliqués, and his arms and legs are jointed for posing.

SOCK CAT

Recycled item: adult-size white tube sock

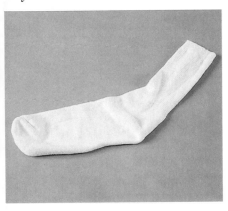

You will also need instant coffee; polyester fiberfill; ecru and black embroidery floss; tracing paper; ecru, pink, and brown felt; drawing compass; soft sculpture needle; four ¹/₂" dia. buttons; 9" of ³/₈"w brown satin ribbon; and a 9mm copper cow bell.

Refer to Embroidery Stitches, page 158, before beginning project.

1. Follow *Coffee Dyeing*, page 156, to dye sock.
2. Refer to Diagram to cut body, legs, and tail from sock. Discard remaining sock pieces.

Diagram

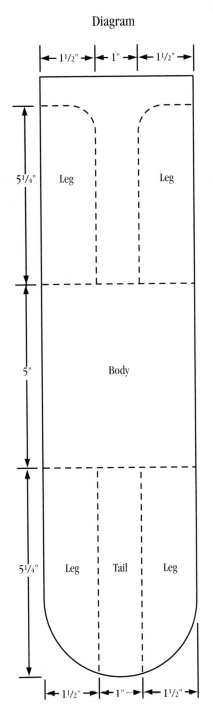

3. Turn body piece wrong side out. Sew edges together at one end. Turn right side out. Refer to Fig. 1 to sew across each corner to form ears. Work a *Running Stitch* along opposite edge of body; do not trim thread ends. Stuff body with fiberfill. Pull thread ends to gather tightly; knot thread ends together. For neck, tie a length of ecru floss around body.

Fig. 1

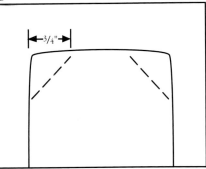

4. For legs and tail, matching right sides and leaving an opening for turning, sew pieces along raw edges. Turn pieces right side out. Stuff each piece with fiberfill. Sew openings closed.
5. Trace muzzle, heart, ears, eyes, stripe, and nose patterns, page 140, onto tracing paper; cut out. Using patterns, cut muzzle, heart, ears, eyes, and four stripes from brown felt and nose from pink felt.
6. Using six strands of ecru floss, work a *Straight Stitch* on each eye. Using six strands of black floss, work a *Backstitch* for mouth and *French Knots* for whiskers on muzzle. Blindstitch shapes to cat.
7. Use compass to draw a 1¹/₂" dia. circle on ecru felt; cut out circle. Blindstitch circle to bottom of body to cover gathers.
8. Use soft sculpture needle and buttons to attach legs to cat. Tack tail to cat.
9. Tie ribbon into a bow around neck. Sew bell to knot of bow.

PILLOW TEES

*N*o one will be able to resist cozying up to these oh-so-soft pillows! They're perfect for relaxing in front of the television or dozing on long trips in the car. A great project for using clothing outgrown by active youngsters, the pillows are made from the most comfortable thing around — T-shirts.

T-SHIRT PILLOWS

Recycled items: T-shirts

You will also need polyester fiberfill and fabric glue.

1. For each pillow, cut hem from bottom of shirt; cut sides from shirt (Fig. 1).

Fig. 1

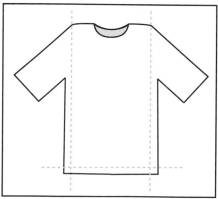

2. Matching right sides and raw edges, use a ¹⁄₄" seam allowance to sew along cut edges. Turn shirt right side out.

3. Stuff pillow through neck opening. Glue neck opening closed; allow to dry.

CHECKERS, ANYONE?

*C*heckers, anyone? Kids will be ready for a game on the go with this soft checkerboard made from time-worn blue jeans. Plastic bottle caps make great playing pieces, and the board can be rolled up for storage.

BLUE JEAN CHECKERBOARD

Recycled items: adult-size pair of blue denim jeans and 26 plastic bottle caps

You will also need straight pins, black acrylic paint, paintbrush, hot glue gun, 3/8"w grosgrain ribbon, and red and black spray paint.

1. For checkerboard, cut eight vertical strips 2³/₄" x 22³/₄" and eight horizontal strips 2³/₄" x 30" from jeans.
2. Securing with pins and with 4" extending at each horizontal side for fringe, weave vertical and horizontal strips together.
3. Excluding fringe and stitching ¹/₄" from outer woven edges, stitch around checkerboard. Remove pins.
4. Paint alternating squares on checkerboard black; allow to dry.
5. Trimming to fit and mitering corners as necessary, glue ribbon around checkerboard.
6. Clip fringe at ¹/₄" to ¹/₂" intervals to ¹/₄" from outer edge of checkerboard.
7. For game pieces, spray paint 13 bottle caps red and 13 bottle caps black.

LITTLE TREASURES

EGG CARTON JEWELRY HOLDER

*H*ere's an "egg-cellent" idea
for storing a little girl's treasures.
Help her turn an ordinary egg carton
into a fanciful trinket box. Simply
spray paint the carton, add designs
with dimensional paint, and top
the box with a colorful bow.

Recycled item: papier-mâché egg carton

You will also need corrugated craft
cardboard; hot glue gun; gold and green
spray paint; yellow, peach, pink, purple,
light green and green dimensional paint;
and 22" of ⁷⁄₈"w purple wired ribbon.

*Refer to Painting Techniques, page 156,
before beginning project. Allow paint to
dry after each application.*

1. Cut two 1¹⁄₂" x 4" pieces from
cardboard. Covering holes, glue pieces to
top of carton with corrugated side up.
2. Spray paint inside and outside of carton
gold. Lightly spray paint outside of
carton green.
3. Use dimensional paint to paint flowers,
leaves, swirls, and dots on carton.
4. Tie ribbon into a bow. Glue bow
to carton.

GLAMOUR GIRL

*D*on't toss out that cache of
hair ribbons your little princess
has stopped wearing — preserve
them on a glamorous photo frame.
Tie the ribbons into bows and
glue the shimmery splashes of
color to an ordinary frame for
an extraordinary keepsake.

RIBBON FRAME

Recycled items: assorted ribbons and a
frame (we used a 5" x 7" frame)
You will also need a hot glue gun.

1. Trimming to fit, glue one length of
ribbon to top, bottom, and each side of
frame front.
2. Tie ribbons into bows. Glue bows
to frame.

PRIMARY COLORS

*T*urn a child's boring bed into a kaleidoscope of fun! Make a padded headboard of crayon shapes with cardboard, fabric bolts, and colorful fabrics to brighten up the room.

CRAYON HEADBOARD

Recycled items: cardboard and 8" x 31" fabric bolts (we used five fabric bolts to make a headboard for a twin-size bed)

You will also need tracing paper, hot glue gun, batting, ¹/₃ yd. each of five solid fabrics in assorted colors, ¹/₂"w and 1"w black grosgrain ribbon, craft knife, cutting mat, and foam core board.

1. Follow *Making Patterns*, page 156, and trace crayon point pattern, page 155, onto tracing paper; cut out. Using pattern, cut five crayon points from cardboard.
2. For each crayon, glue one crayon point across one short end of one fabric bolt. Cut one 10" x 40" piece each from batting and fabric. Wrapping to back and clipping as necessary, wrap and glue batting, then fabric around crayon.

3. Overlapping ends at back, glue one 1"w length and two ¹/₂"w lengths of ribbon around crayon below point.

4. Use craft knife to cut a 29" x 36¹/₂" piece of foam core board. Arrange and glue crayons on foam core board.

TRAVEL-TIME FUN

*H*eaded out on a road trip?
*Don't forget to pack this travel-time
tote — it helps pass the miles with
toys, games, and snacks! A fold-up
cardboard beverage carrier is
transformed using vibrant fabrics,
rickrack, and buttons.*

TRIP TOTE

Recycled item: cardboard beverage
carrier that can be unfolded to lay flat

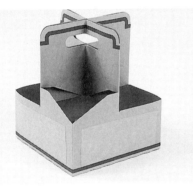

You will also need two coordinating
fabrics, spray adhesive, cutting mat, craft
knife, craft glue, jumbo rickrack, hot glue
gun, and assorted buttons.

1. Carefully disassemble carrier. Cut a
piece from each fabric 1" larger on all
sides than unfolded carrier.
2. Apply spray adhesive to one side of
carrier. Place one fabric piece wrong side
up on cutting mat. Center carrier on
fabric; press firmly to secure. Use craft
knife to cut fabric even with edges of
carrier. If carrier has slits, use craft knife
to cut through slits.
3. Applying spray adhesive to remaining
side of carrier and using remaining fabric
piece, repeat Step 2 to cover remaining
side of carrier. Use craft glue to
reassemble carrier; allow to dry.

4. Measure around carrier; add ¹/₂". Cut
a length of rickrack the determined
measurement. Overlapping ends, hot glue
rickrack around carrier. Hot glue buttons
to rickrack.

"A-HEAD" OF THE BAND

Rummaging through drawers to find lost hair accessories is now a thing of the past! A large cardboard container becomes a useful headband holder when embellished with fabric, ribbon, and a button, and there's lots of room inside for barrettes.

HEADBAND HOLDER

Recycled item: 5" dia. cardboard container with a lid

You will also need white spray primer, assorted fabrics, spray adhesive, jumbo rickrack, hot glue gun, drawing compass, 18" of 1½"w grosgrain ribbon, tracing paper, and a button.

1. Remove lid from container. Apply primer to container; allow to dry.
2. Measure around container; add ½". Measure height of container between rims. Cut a piece from fabric the determined measurements. Apply spray adhesive to wrong side of fabric piece. Position and smooth fabric piece around container.
3. Measure around container; add ½". Cut two lengths from rickrack the determined measurement. Overlapping ends at back, glue rickrack around top and bottom of container.
4. Measure diameter of lid; multiply by 2. Using compass, draw a circle on wrong side of fabric the determined measurement. Follow Steps 2 and 3 of *Making a Fabric Yo-Yo*, page 159, to finish edge of circle. Place lid bottom side down at center of circle. Pull ends of thread to tightly gather circle over lid; knot thread ends together to secure.
5. Using ribbon, follow *Making a Ruched Flower*, page 158, to make ribbon flower. Glue ribbon flower over center gathers on lid.
6. For fabric flower, use compass to draw a 3½" circle on tracing paper; cut out. Using pattern, follow *Making a Fabric Yo-Yo* to make flower. Sew button to center of flower. Glue fabric flower over center gathers of ribbon flower.

CLOWNING AROUND

*P*ut a twist on a favorite children's party game with this festive cookie sheet clown. His cheery face is painted in bright colors, and magnets provide a safe way for kids to "pin" on the pom-pom nose.

COOKIE SHEET CLOWN

Recycled item: metal cookie sheet large enough to accommodate a 10" dia. circle (make sure magnets will stick to your cookie sheet before beginning project)

You will also need sandpaper; tack cloth; grey spray primer; drawing compass; white, yellow, red, blue, and black acrylic paint; paintbrushes; tracing paper; transfer paper; ³/₄" dia. to 1¹/₄" dia. round foam brushes; hot glue gun; ³/₄" dia. magnet for each nose; 2" dia. red pom-pom for each nose; and 30" of 1"w red polka-dot ribbon.

Allow primer and paint to dry after each application.

1. Sand cookie sheet. Use tack cloth to remove dust. Apply primer to cookie sheet.
2. For head, use compass to draw a 10" dia. circle on cookie sheet. Paint head white.

3. Trace patterns, pages 138 and 139, onto tracing paper. Use transfer paper to transfer face, hair, and bow tie to head. Paint face, hair, and bow tie. Use round foam brushes to add nose and dots.
4. For each "nose" game piece, glue one magnet to one pom-pom.

5. For hanger, cut 10" from ribbon. Glue ends to back of cookie sheet. Tie remaining ribbon into a bow. Glue to front of cookie sheet.

COLLEGE BOUND

Teens will enjoy "stuffing" their dirty clothes in this hanging laundry tote, especially if it's made from a T-shirt that sports their school logo. What a great gift idea for college-bound grads!

T-SHIRT LAUNDRY BAG

Recycled items: T-shirt and a hanger

1. Cut sides from shirt (Fig. 1).

Fig. 1

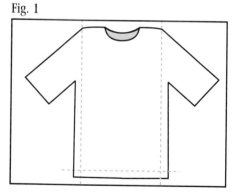

2. Matching right sides and raw edges, use a $1/4$" seam allowance and sew along sides and bottom of shirt. Turn shirt right side out.

3. For laundry bag, insert hanger in neck of shirt.

52

LOCKER PAL

*W*hat student wouldn't appreciate a way to get organized? Our inventive locker caddy is ideal for boys or girls. Four blue-jeans pockets provide spots for pencils, scissors, notes, and more!

BLUE JEAN POCKET ORGANIZER

Recycled items: two pairs of denim jeans with back pockets

You will also need heavy-duty paper-backed fusible web, 7" x 29" piece of foam core board, hot glue gun, 72" of welting with lip, and 83" of jute twine.

1. Beginning 1³/₄" above back pocket, cut an 8" x 30" piece from one leg of one pair of jeans. Cut a 7" x 29" piece of web. Cutting completely through jeans, cut remaining back pockets from both pairs of jeans.

2. For background, center and fuse web to wrong side of 8" x 30" jean piece. Arrange jean piece web side down on foam core board; fuse in place. Glue ends to back of foam core board.

3. With right sides up, draw around each pocket on paper side of web; cut out and fuse to wrong side of pockets. Arrange and fuse pockets to background.

4. Beginning and ending at center bottom, follow *Adding Welting*, page 159, to glue welting along edges of organizer.

5. Beginning 5¹/₂" from one end of twine and beginning and ending at center top, glue twine along edges of organizer.

6. Knot ends of twine together for hanger.

GARDENER'S TREASURES

Gardening is a wonderful hobby, providing beauty and rejuvenation for both the gardener and the earth. Why not do nature a favor and recycle items headed for the waste bin into great crafts! You can make a unique planter from an old pair of blue jeans or a broken chair. Breathe new life into an outdoor glider with a fresh coat of paint and simple floral designs, or salvage an old wooden column and a battered wash basin to create a pretty birdbath. Green-thumbed friends will love bright garden stakes or a cute "Welcome" sign with soda-can characters! Whether you're decorating a backyard oasis or your living room, you'll pick a bushel of clever accents from this inventive section!

"DAISY" DAYS

Enjoy the "daisy" days of summer in a garden seat built for two! An ordinary metal glider is transformed into a lovely outdoor accessory with a coat of pastel paint and simple stenciled flowers.

GLIDER

Recycled item: metal glider

You will also need items listed under *Preparing an Item for Painting* (page 156); grey spray primer; kraft paper; masking tape; light green and purple spray paint; stencil plastic; craft knife; cutting mat; white, yellow, and green acrylic latex enamel paint; stencil brushes; 3/4" dia. round foam brushes; and a black permanent fine-point marker.

Allow primer and paint to dry after each application.

1. Follow *Preparing an Item for Painting*, page 156, to prepare glider.
2. Apply primer to glider.
3. Use kraft paper and masking tape to cover seat and back of glider. Spray paint handles purple. Use kraft paper and

masking tape to cover handles. Spray paint seat and back green.
4. Using daisy pattern, page 140, and following *Stenciling*, page 157, stencil white petals and green stems and leaves on seat.
5. Use round foam brushes to paint yellow flower centers and dots. Use marker to outline flower centers as desired.

THE BEST SEAT IN THE HOUSE

*G*ive your flowers the best seat in the house! Our painted flowerpot chair is sure to spark conversation among your friends — especially those with green thumbs. We decorated an old wooden chair with various painted designs and placed the pot where a rattan seat cover once stretched over the opening.

FLOWERPOT CHAIR

Recycled item: wooden chair with broken caned seat

You will also need items listed under *Preparing an Item for Painting* (page 156), white spray primer, assorted colors of acrylic paint (we used light yellow, light purple, grey blue, and light green), paintbrushes, tracing paper, transfer paper, purple and green permanent medium-point markers, matte acrylic spray sealer, and a clay flowerpot to fit in hole of seat.

Allow primer, paint, and sealer to dry after each application.

1. Follow *Preparing an Item for Painting*, page 156, to prepare chair.
2. Apply primer to chair. Paint desired colors on chair (we painted sections of the legs and uprights alternating colors and a 1³/₄" x 8⁵/₈" rectangle on top rung of chair).
3. Trace patterns, page 141, onto tracing paper. Use transfer paper to transfer words and vines to rungs of chair. Use markers to draw over words and vines.
4. Apply two to three coats of sealer to chair.

5. Mix one part desired color of paint with one part water. Paint flowerpot with paint mixture.

6. If necessary, cut an opening in seat large enough to accommodate flowerpot. Place flowerpot through seat of chair.

BEAUTY BATH

Perfect for bird lovers, this project is a luxurious invitation for feathered friends to visit. We used a pair of half-columns taken from a fireplace mantel and an old enamel wash basin to begin the assembly of this "beauty bath." Create the finishing touches by sponge-painting greenery and flowers.

BIRDBATH

Recycled items: one column or two half-columns (we used two half-columns from a fireplace mantel) and an enamel wash pan

You will also need items listed under *Preparing an Item for Painting* (page 156), household cement, wood putty, fine-grit sandpaper, tack cloth, rectangular wooden plaque large enough to accommodate bottom of columns, circular wooden plaque large enough to cover top of columns, craft drill, ¹/₂"l wood screws, white spray primer, white spray paint, pink and green acrylic paint, household sponge, paintbrushes, and clear acrylic spray sealer.

Instructions are written using two half-columns. Refer to Painting Techniques, page 156, before beginning project. Allow household cement, wood putty, primer, paint, and sealer to dry after each application.

1. Follow *Preparing an Item for Painting*, page 156, to prepare columns.
2. Glue columns together. If necessary, fill crack between columns with wood putty; use sandpaper to smooth. Remove dust with tack cloth.
3. Glue rectangular plaque to bottom and circular plaque to top of columns. Use craft drill to make four pilot holes through rectangular plaque and into bottom of columns. Use craft drill to make four pilot holes through circular plaque and into top of columns. Use screws to secure plaques to columns.
4. For birdbath, glue wash pan to circular plaque.
5. Apply primer to birdbath. Spray paint birdbath white.
6. Sponge paint leaves and flowers on birdbath. Paint vine and grass on birdbath.
7. Apply two to three coats of sealer to birdbath.

AUTUMN WELCOME

Welcome autumn and all your fall-loving friends with this whimsical fence-post scarecrow. His timeworn clothes cover a fence-picket body and broom-handle arms, and his friendly face is painted on a brown paper bag.

SCARECROW FENCE POST

Recycled items: wooden broom handle, flannel shirt, pair of denim jeans, 33" of rope, brown paper bag, and a straw hat

You will also need a handsaw; 6-foot fence picket; craft drill; two 1¹/₂"l bolts with nuts; staple gun; orange, pink, and black acrylic paint; paintbrushes; natural raffia; hot glue gun; 4"h artificial blackbird; and an artificial flower.

1. Use handsaw to cut 12" from top of picket and cut broom handle to measure 38".
2. For arms, drilling holes side-by-side and measuring 16" from top of picket, drill two holes 2" apart in picket. Drill two holes 2" apart in center of broom handle. Forming a T-shape, use bolts to attach broom handle to picket.

3. For scarecrow, place shirt on arms. Gather shirt at "waist"; staple excess shirt to back of picket. Roll up sleeves of shirt.
4. Cut a slit large enough to insert picket between back pockets of jeans. Slide picket through slit. Gathering jeans with rope, tuck shirt tail into jeans. Staple waist of jeans to back of picket. Roll up legs of jeans; staple to front of picket.
5. For head, paint face on paper bag; allow to dry. Lightly crumple bag, then smooth out. Place bag over top of picket. Secure bag at neck with a length of raffia.
6. For each "straw" bundle, fold several lengths of raffia in half; fold in half again.

Continue folding and adding more raffia until desired thickness is achieved. Tie a length of raffia around one end of bundle; trim opposite end to desired length. Repeat to make a total of five "straw" bundles for hair, hands, and feet.
7. Glue one bundle to top of head for hair. Glue folded end of one bundle inside each sleeve opening for hands and inside each leg opening for feet. Stuff raffia into pockets and inside shirt collar.
8. Glue blackbird to arm. Glue flower to hat, then hat to head.

GARDEN COMPANION

*Y*ou'll reap a bushel of ideas with this personal gardening journal. It's perfect for recording what you've planted and harvested each season. The delightful cover is decorated with "recycled" veggie can labels.

GARDENING JOURNAL

Recycled items: vegetable can labels and a twig

You will also need tracing paper, yellow and dark yellow card stock, craft glue, spiral-bound journal, green permanent medium-point marker, foam brush, garden clippers, and natural raffia.

1. Trace sun and sun rays patterns, page 148, onto tracing paper; cut out. Using patterns, cut sun from yellow card stock and sun rays from dark yellow card stock. Glue sun rays, then sun to front of journal; allow to dry. Use marker to write "My Gardening Journal" on sun.

2. Cut desired motifs from labels. Mix one part glue with one part water. Use foam brush to apply glue mixture to back of motifs. Arrange motifs on journal; smooth in place. Apply glue mixture over motifs; allow to dry.

3. Measure height of journal. Use garden clippers to cut a length from twig the determined measurement. Use several lengths of raffia to tie twig to journal binding.

SPRING HAS SPRUNG

*A*dd a bit of springtime fun to your flowerbed or garden with inventive rebar stakes. (If you've done any home-construction projects using concrete, you probably have some rebar stakes left over.) The blooms and leaves are cut from aluminum cans and painted. Choose a daisy or a sunflower, or display both for a splash of color all year 'round!

GARDEN STAKES

Recycled items: 12-oz. aluminum beverage cans and assorted buttons

You will also need utility scissors; white spray primer; white, yellow, green, and brown acrylic paint; paintbrushes; hammer; nail; wire cutters; medium-gauge craft wire; hot glue gun; 24" rebar stake; tracing paper; and clear acrylic spray sealer.

Allow primer, paint, and sealer to dry after each application.

SUNFLOWER STAKE

1. For flower pieces, use utility scissors to cut through opening of two beverage cans; cut away and discard tops. Beginning at cut edge and cutting to within $^1/_2$" of bottom of can, cut down sides of each can at $^5/_8$" to $1^1/_4$" intervals to make petals. Flatten each can with petals extending outward. Trim end of each petal to a point.
2. Apply primer to each side of each flower piece. Paint both sides of each flower piece yellow.
3. For flower center, paint inside bottom of one flower piece brown. For each "seed," use hammer and nail to punch two holes for each button along edge of flower center. Thread button onto a 4" length of wire, then wire ends through holes in flower center. Twist at back to secure.
4. Glue flower piece with "seeds" over remaining flower piece.
5. Punching through both layers, use hammer and nail to punch two holes in center of flower. Thread button onto a 6" length of wire, then wire ends through holes in flower center. Twist wire ends around rebar to secure.
6. For leaves, use utility scissors to cut through opening and down to bottom of two beverage cans; cut away and discard tops and bottoms of cans. Flatten each can piece. Apply primer to both sides of each can piece. Paint both sides of each can piece green.

7. Trace large leaf pattern, page 150, onto tracing paper; cut out. Using pattern, cut two leaves from green can pieces. Use hammer and nail to punch two sets of two holes in each leaf. Use wire to attach leaves to rebar through holes.
8. Apply two to three coats of sealer to stake.

DAISY STAKE

1. Rounding each petal, follow Step 1 of Sunflower Stake to make flower pieces.
2. Apply primer to both sides of each flower piece. Paint both sides of each flower piece white.
3. For flower center, paint inside bottom of one flower piece yellow. Glue flower piece with center over remaining flower piece. Punching through both layers, use hammer and nail to punch four holes in flower center. Forming an "X," thread ends of two 7" lengths of wire through holes in flower center. Twist wire ends around rebar to secure.
4. For leaf, use utility scissors to cut through opening and down to bottom of one beverage can; cut away and discard top and bottom of can. Flatten can piece. Apply primer to both sides of can piece. Paint both sides of can piece green.
5. Trace small leaf pattern, page 150, onto tracing paper; cut out. Using pattern, cut leaf from green can piece. Use hammer and nail to punch two sets of two holes in leaf. Use wire to attach leaf to rebar through holes.
6. Apply two to three coats of sealer to stake.

GARDEN MASTERPIECE

*Y*ou can transform an ordinary wooden folding chair into a garden masterpiece with pretty hand-painted designs. We chose flowers and a bee, but the decorative possibilities are endless!

FOLDING CHAIR

Recycled item: wooden folding chair

You will also need items listed under *Preparing an Item for Painting* (page 156), white spray primer, assorted colors of acrylic paint, paintbrushes, black permanent medium-point marker, and clear acrylic spray sealer.

Allow primer, paint, and sealer to dry after each application.

1. Follow *Preparing an Item for Painting*, page 156, to prepare chair.
2. Apply primer to chair. Paint desired base coats on chair (we painted the chair frame and seat back white and remaining sections of the chair in contrasting colors).
3. Paint designs on chair (we painted flowers and a bumblebee). Use marker to add detail lines to designs.
4. Apply two to three coats of sealer to chair.

BLOOMING BEAUTY

Blooming beauties will look even lovelier in this embellished flowerpot. Faux leaves cover the container, and a rose-bedecked bow gives it Victorian flair.

EVERGREEN FLOWERPOT

Recycled item: flowerpot
You will also need artificial leaves and flowers, hot glue gun, and 15" of ⅝"w wired ribbon.

1. With tips of leaves extending above flowerpot and overlapping as necessary, glue right sides of leaves around inside rim of flowerpot.
2. With tips of leaves extending above flowerpot and overlapping as necessary, glue wrong sides of leaves around outside rim of flowerpot.
3. Covering entire flowerpot and overlapping as necessary, layer and glue leaves to flowerpot.
4. Tie ribbon into a bow. Glue bow, then flowers to flowerpot.

"UN-BEE-LIEVABLE" BIRDHOUSE

*T*he neighbors will never "bee-lieve" that this whimsical birdhouse is made from items that were destined for the trash! Hang it in a sunny window for a fun focal point.

BUMBLEBEE BIRDHOUSE

Recycled items: 18-oz. cardboard oatmeal container with lid for body, two wire hangers, and window screen

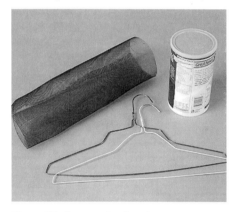

You will also need a drawing compass; craft knife; cutting mat; wire cutters; pliers; white, yellow, and black acrylic paint; paintbrushes; two ³/₄" dia. wooden beads; 4" dia. papier-mâché ball for head; tracing paper; transfer paper; push pin; hot glue gun; heavy gloves; medium-gauge craft wire; and natural raffia.

Allow paint to dry after each application. Use pliers to shape wire.

1. Remove lid from container. Using compass, draw a 1" dia. circle on lid near rim. Use craft knife to carefully cut out circle. Replace lid.
2. Use wire cutters to cut six 3¹/₂" lengths from hangers for legs, two 3" lengths for antennae, one 2" length for stinger, and one 14" length for hanger.

3. Shape each wire for legs into a Z-shape. Shape antennae as desired.
4. Paint body and wooden beads yellow and head, legs, antennae, and stinger black.
5. Trace face pattern, page 153, onto tracing paper. Use transfer paper to transfer face to head. Paint face. Paint stripes and details on body.
6. Using push pin to make pilot holes, make two holes in head for antennae and one hole each in body for hanger, stinger, and legs.
7. Apply glue to one end of each leg and stinger; insert in body. Apply glue to one end of each antennae; insert ends into

beads. Apply glue to opposite ends of antennae; insert into head. Glue head to body.
8. For wings, use wire cutters to cut a 8¹/₂" x 14" oval from screen. Wearing gloves, fold edges ¹/₄" to wrong side twice. Gather screen at center; secure with wire.
9. Work one end of wire for hanger through gathers of wings; bend end into L-shape. Apply glue to wire end; insert in body. Shape remaining end of hanger into a U-shape.
10. Tie several lengths of raffia into a bow around neck.

JUST "IN-JEAN-IOUS"

*D*on't throw away those old blue jeans! We've found a fun and easy way to make them into a useful garden accessory. Create the unique planter by removing the legs of denim jeans and belting the waist around a clay pot. Miniature gardening tools and seed packets add a "home-grown" touch.

BLUE JEAN PLANTER

Recycled items: adult-size pair of denim jeans with front pockets and a belt

You will also need an 8½" dia. clay flowerpot with saucer, green raffia, miniature gardening tools, and seed packets.

1. Cut legs from jeans; discard legs.
2. Matching right sides, sew leg openings closed. Turn jeans right side out.
3. Place flowerpot with saucer in jeans. Thread belt through belt loops and tightly cinch belt around flowerpot to secure.
4. Tie several lengths of raffia around tool handles. Place tools and seed packets in jeans pockets.

FOOD CAN WIND CHIMES

Bring harmony to your backyard paradise with these colorful wind chimes. Empty food cans are strung together with beads and wire to jingle in the breeze. Brush on simple painted patterns for an eye-pleasing outdoor accent.

Recycled items: three food cans in graduated sizes, one top from can, and assorted beads

You will also need white spray primer; green spray paint; light orange, orange, light green, and green acrylic paint; paintbrushes; clear acrylic spray sealer; hammer; nail; gold eye pins; 36" of heavy-gauge craft wire; and pliers.

Refer to Painting Techniques, page 156, before beginning project. Allow primer, paint, and sealer to dry after each application. Use pliers to bend wire.

1. Apply primer to cans and both sides of can top. Spray paint cans and both sides of can top green.
2. Use acrylic paint to paint designs on cans and can top (we painted stripes, dots, and wavy lines on our cans and spatter painted one can). Apply two to three coats of sealer to cans and can top.
3. Use hammer and nail to punch holes at 1/2" intervals 1/4" from rim around open edge of smallest can, one hole in center bottom of each can, and one hole 1/4" from edge in can top.
4. For hanging beads, thread several beads onto eye pins. Insert straight ends of eye pins through holes around open edge in smallest can. Bend ends to inside of can to secure.
5. For clapper, thread 2" of wire through hole in can top. Twist wire end to secure.
6. Thread several beads onto wire.
7. Working inside to outside, thread wire through bottom of smallest can. Mark wire at desired placement for top of can; remove can. Thread one bead onto wire. Holding bead on wire where marked, wrap wire around and back through bead (Fig. 1). Replace can over bead. Repeat to add medium and large cans on wire.

Fig. 1

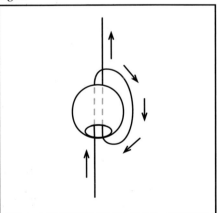

8. Thread two beads onto wire. For hanger, bend wire end into a loop.

HIGH FLYING CONDO

BIRDHOUSE CONDO

Refer to Painting Techniques, page 156, before beginning project. Allow primer and paint to dry after each application. Use garden clippers to cut twigs.

BLUE BIRDHOUSE
Recycled items: large paper carton at least 3³/₄" x 10", twigs, two 12-oz. aluminum beverage cans, and a foam food tray
You will also need a hot glue gun; white spray primer; gold, light blue, and blue acrylic paint; paintbrushes; household sponge; drawing compass; craft knife; cutting mat; push pin; garden clippers; utility scissors; crimping tool; tracing paper; Spanish moss; and grapevine.

1. Use hot glue to reseal carton. Apply three coats of primer to outside of carton.
2. For birdhouse, paint carton blue. Cut a 1" square piece from sponge. Sponge paint a light blue checkerboard design on birdhouse.
3. Using compass, draw two 1" dia. circles 3" apart on one side of birdhouse. Use craft knife to carefully cut out openings.

4. For each perch, use push pin to make a pilot hole ¹/₄" below each opening. Cut a 1¹/₂" long twig; insert in hole.
5. Use utility scissors to cut through opening and down to bottom of each beverage can; cut top and bottom from each can. Flatten cans.
6. For roof panels, refer to Fig. 1 to measure width and height of roof; add ¹/₂" to each measurement. Cut two pieces from flattened cans the determined measurements. Use crimping tool to crimp can pieces. Bend one long edge of each can piece ¹/₂" to printed side. Overlapping as necessary, glue bends in roof panels over top of birdhouse.

Fig. 1

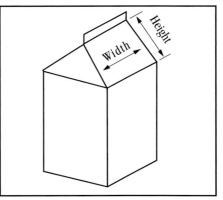

7. Trace star pattern, page 135, onto tracing paper; cut out. Using pattern and craft knife, cut star from foam food tray. Paint star gold.
8. Glue star to birdhouse between openings. Glue moss and grapevine to openings and eaves of roof.

For some high-flying fun, add this colorful "condo" to your sunroom decor. Constructed from paper cartons, the trio of birdhouses is topped with "tin" roofs fashioned from beverage cans. The cute polka-dot bird is cut from a foam food tray!

GREEN BIRDHOUSE

Recycled items: one medium-size paper carton at least 2¾" x 8", twigs, 12-oz. aluminum beverage can, and a foam food tray

You will also need a hot glue gun; white spray primer; white, red, and green acrylic paint; paintbrushes; household sponge; drawing compass; craft knife; cutting mat; push pin; garden clippers; utility scissors; crimping tool; tracing paper; Spanish moss; and grapevine.

1. Follow Step 1 of Blue Birdhouse to prepare carton.

2. For birdhouse, paint carton green. Cut a ½" x 1¼" piece from sponge. Sponge paint white "bricks" on corners of birdhouse.

3. Using compass, draw three ¾" dia. circles ½" apart on one side of birdhouse. Use craft knife to carefully cut out openings.

4. For each perch, follow Step 4 of Blue Birdhouse to insert one perch under each opening. Follow Step 5 to prepare can.

5. For roof panel, refer to Fig. 1 to measure width and height of roof; add ½" to each measurement. Multiply height measurement by 2. Cut a piece from flattened can the determined measurements. Use crimping tool to crimp can piece. Center roof panel on top of roof and glue to birdhouse.

6. Trace small heart pattern, page 135, onto tracing paper; cut out. Using pattern and craft knife, cut heart from foam food tray. Paint heart red.

7. Glue heart to birdhouse above openings. Glue moss and grapevine to openings and eaves of roof.

RED BIRDHOUSE

Recycled items: one small paper carton at least 2¾" x 5¾", twig, 12-oz. aluminum beverage can, and a foam food tray

You will also need a hot glue gun; white spray primer; white, red, blue, and brown acrylic paint; paintbrushes; household sponge; drawing compass; craft knife; cutting mat; push pin; garden clippers; utility scissors; crimping tool; tracing paper; Spanish moss; and grapevine.

1. Follow Step 1 of Blue Birdhouse to prepare carton.

2. For birdhouse, paint carton red. Cut two ½" x 1" pieces from sponge. Sponge paint brown "bricks" on birdhouse. Sponge paint white highlights on "bricks."

3. Using compass, draw a 1" dia. circle ¾" from bottom of birdhouse. Use craft knife to carefully cut out opening.

4. Follow Steps 4 and 5 of Green Birdhouse to make perch and roof.

5. Trace large heart pattern, page 135, onto tracing paper; cut out. Using pattern and craft knife, cut heart from foam food tray. Paint heart blue.

6. Glue heart to birdhouse above opening. Glue moss and grapevine to opening and eaves of roof.

BIRDHOUSE CONDO

Recycled items: large coffee can, tree limb, brown paper bag, two 12-oz. aluminum beverage cans, foam food tray, and a twig

You will also need plaster of paris, hot glue gun, Spanish moss, utility scissors, crimping tool, natural raffia, gold and black acrylic paint, paintbrushes, 8" square of foam core board, white paint pen, craft knife, cutting mat, Blue Birdhouse, Green Birdhouse, Red Birdhouse, tracing paper, garden clippers, grapevine, and silk flowers.

1. Follow manufacturer's instructions to prepare plaster. Fill coffee can to within 1½" of top with plaster. Insert one end of tree limb in center of can. Allow plaster to harden.

2. Pleating paper as necessary, wrap can with brown paper bag; glue top edges to inside of can. Fill can with moss.

3. Use utility scissors to cut through opening and down to bottom of beverage cans; cut top and bottom from cans. Flatten can pieces.

4. Measure around coffee can. Piecing as necessary, cut a strip from can pieces 1¾"w by the determined measurement. Use crimping tool to crimp can strip. Glue can strip around center of coffee can. Tie several lengths of raffia into a knot around coffee can.

5. For platform, paint foam core board gold. Paint ½" black squares along edges of platform. Use paint pen to outline squares.

6. Use craft knife to cut an "X" in center of platform slightly smaller than diameter of tree limb. Arrange and glue birdhouses to platform around "X." Apply glue to remaining end of limb. Insert end of limb through "X" in platform.

7. Trace bird and wing patterns, page 135, onto tracing paper; cut out. Using patterns and craft knife, cut bird and wing from foam food tray.

8. Paint bird and wing black; paint beak and eye gold. Use white paint pen to add white dots to bird and wing. Glue wing to bird. Cut a 4¼" long twig. Glue bird to twig.

9. Apply glue to opposite end of twig. Glue twig, moss, grapevine, and silk flowers to condo.

HARVEST HOME

*P*ost this folksy sign in the dining room, and your guests will know that the bounty they're enjoying comes from your garden. Twigs frame the inviting message, and buttons and a plaid ribbon hanger enhance its homey charm.

GARDEN SAMPLER

Recycled items: brown paper bag, 6" x 12½" shoe box lid, and twigs

You will also need tracing paper, transfer paper, green permanent fine-point marker, hot glue gun, garden clippers, buttons, moss, and fabric.

1. For sampler, cut a 4½" x 11" piece from bag. Matching grey lines and arrows, trace design, page 136, onto tracing paper. Use transfer paper to transfer design to center of bag piece. Use marker to draw over transferred lines. Center and glue sampler on top of shoe box lid.

2. For "frame," use garden clippers to cut two 8" lengths and two 11" lengths from twigs. Glue 11" twig lengths along top and bottom, then 8" twig lengths along sides of sampler. Cut enough 2½" lengths of remaining twigs to cover outer edges of sampler. Glue twigs around sampler.

3. Glue buttons and moss to sampler.

4. For hanger, tear a 1¼" x 18" piece from fabric. Glue ends of strip to back of sampler. Glue button to center of strip.

IMAGINATIVE PLANTER

*L*et your imagination take root
with this no-fuss planter. To make it,
brown paper bags are simply sponge-
painted, rolled into tubes, and glued
to a coffee can. Faux metallic bands
add a final decorative touch.

COFFEE CAN PLANTER

Recycled items: three large brown paper
bags and a 6³⁄₄"h coffee can with a 6" dia.
opening

You will also need gold, copper, and
turquoise acrylic paint; natural sponge;
paintbrush; and a hot glue gun.

*Refer to Painting Techniques, page 156,
before beginning project. Allow paint to
dry after each application.*

1. Cut each bag open along one fold
and cut away bottom; press with a warm,
dry iron.
2. For bands, cut two 1" x 23" strips
from bag. Sponge paint strips gold, then
copper.
3. Remove lid from can. Paint both sides
of remaining bags and inside of can
turquoise. Sponge paint one side of bags
and inside of can copper.

4. Cut fifty-five 2" x 7" strips from
remaining bags. With sponge- painted
side to outside, wrap each paper bag strip
around a pencil; glue seam to secure.
Remove pencil.
5. Glue tubes, then bands around can.

NATURAL STARS

TWIG STAR PLANT POKES

You can collect the items you need to make these primitive plant pokes while taking a stroll through the backyard! Crafted from twigs, berries, and pinecones, the simple accents are sure to transform your potted plants into "star" attractions.

Recycled Items: twigs

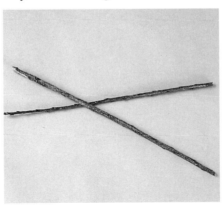

You will also need garden clippers, hot glue gun, jute twine, and items to decorate pokes (we used a strip of fabric, natural raffia, small pinecones, artificial berries, and a button).

Use garden clippers to cut twigs.

1. For each plant poke, cut five 8½" lengths and one 18" length from twigs.
2. Referring to Fig. 1, glue twigs together to form plant poke.

Fig. 1

3. Wrapping in a crisscross direction, wrap twine around twigs at star points and center intersections.
4. Glue decorative items to plant poke as desired.

*G*reet guests with the funny-face frogs on our cute "Welcome" sign. Aluminum cans are "recycled" to make the frogs' bodies and crimped legs.

CRUSHED CAN FROGS

Recycled items: five 12-oz. aluminum beverage cans and four metal bottle caps

You will also need utility scissors; paper crimping tool; tracing paper; black permanent medium-point marker; white spray primer; green spray paint; white, red, and black acrylic paint; paintbrushes; household cement; 6¹/₂" x 10¹/₄" piece of corrugated cardboard; green highlighter; push pin; two 20" lengths of jute twine; and two ⁷/₈" dia. green buttons.

Allow primer, paint, and household cement to dry after each application.

1. For frog bodies, remove tabs from two cans. For each can, use both hands to hold can with thumbs below top rim and opening. Using thumbs, press on can to bend top rim down. Turn can upside down and repeat to bend bottom of can in opposite direction. Step on can to flatten further (Fig. 1).

Fig. 1

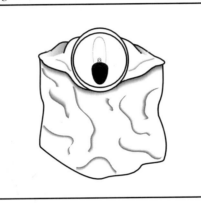

2. Use utility scissors to cut through opening and down to bottom of remaining beverage cans; cut top and bottom from each can. Flatten each can piece.
3. For hind legs, cut four ³/₄" x 8¹/₄" strips from one can piece. For forelegs, cut four ¹/₂" x 8¹/₄" strips from second can piece. Use crimping tool to crimp strips.

4. Trace foot pattern, page 152, onto tracing paper; cut out. Use marker to draw around pattern eight times on remaining can piece. Cut out feet.
5. Spray all sides of bodies, legs, feet, and bottle caps with primer, then green paint. For each mouth, paint inside of each body at opening red. For eyes, paint inside of each bottle cap black with two white highlights.
6. Glue feet to legs. Glue legs and eyes to bodies.
7. For sign, use marker to write "Welcome to My Pad" and add details along edges of cardboard. Use highlighter to accent words.
8. Arrange and glue each frog to sign.
9. For hanger, use push pin to make a pilot hole 1¹/₂" from each side at top of sign.
10. Working from back of sign, thread one end of each length of twine through one hole in sign, then through holes in buttons; knot ends of twine together to secure. Repeat with remaining ends.

FLEA MARKET FINDS

Flea markets are a haven of treasures, especially when those finds are enhanced with these lovely ideas! Whether it's battered furniture, a weathered window frame, or faded plastic dishes, give it the Midas touch for a keepsake more precious than gold. In this section, memories are displayed and games are played in the light of our novel lamps. Nature is celebrated both within the home and out in the garden with a variety of projects, such as a fountain, a planter, and a rug. No matter what you manage to scavenge up, we'll help you spice it up!

WINDOW OF MEMORIES

*E*xpensive store-bought photo holders don't have the same memorable touch as this homey frame. Made from an old window frame, it opens up windows of memories!

WINDOWPANE FRAME

Recycled item: 4-pane window

You will also need items listed under *Preparing an Item for Painting* (page 156), kraft paper, masking tape, white spray primer, white spray paint, black acrylic paint, paintbrush, black permanent medium-point marker, craft knife, cutting mat, mat board, double-sided transparent tape, desired photographs, colored pencils, tracing paper, transfer paper, poster board, and a hot glue gun.

Allow primer and paint to dry after each application.

1. Follow *Preparing an Item for Painting*, page 156, to prepare frame.
2. Use kraft paper and masking tape to cover window panes. Apply primer to window frame. Spray paint window frame white. Paint evenly spaced black squares around edges of window. Use marker to outline squares. Remove kraft paper and masking tape.
3. Use craft knife to cut a piece of mat board to fit inside each pane. Using double-sided tape, position and tape desired photographs on mat board pieces. Use marker to outline photographs as desired.
4. Using colored pencils, draw a scalloped border around outer edges of mat board pieces.
5. Trace Flower A, Flower B, Flower C, and Flower D patterns, page 149, onto tracing paper. Use transfer paper to transfer flowers around photographs as desired. Use marker to outline flowers. Use colored pencils to color flowers and add detail lines to mat board (we added wavy lines around several of our flowers).
6. Mount mat board pieces in window frames.
7. Use transfer paper to transfer Flower D desired number of times to poster board. Use marker to outline flowers. Use colored pencils to color flowers. Cut out flowers. Glue flowers to window as desired.

SEASIDE TABLE

Sand, seashells, fish netting, and knickknacks capture summer memories in this creative coffee table. Transform an old display case into a keepsake by adding legs and then weathering it with our whitewash technique.

SHOWCASE COFFEE TABLE

Recycled item: display case with a hinged, glass top

You will also need items listed under *Preparing an Item for Painting* (page 156), four table leg mounting brackets, four 14" table legs, fine-grit sandpaper, tack cloth, white and blue acrylic paint, paintbrushes, paste floor wax, hot glue gun, and items to place in display case (we used sand, seashells, decorative wooden fish, scraps of fish netting, greenery, and photographs).

1. Follow *Preparing an Item for Painting*, page 156, to prepare display case.
2. For table, follow manufacturer's instructions and use mounting brackets to attach legs to display case.
3. Painting a blue base coat on table, follow *Weathered Whitewash Technique*, page 157, to paint table.
4. Paint latch on display case white; allow to dry. If desired, glue decorative item to top of latch.
5. Arrange decorative items in display case; spot glue as necessary to secure.

TOPIARY TREASURE

*D*isplaying *favorite collectibles is a great way to decorate a home, and this fun fix-up provides a place to show off your treasures. We refinished an old cabinet and table with crackled paint and a sponge-painted topiary.*

TOPIARY CABINET

Recycled item: hutch with shelves (we used a 22^1/$_2$"w x 40"h hutch)
You will also need items listed under *Preparing an Item for Painting* (page 156); table large enough to accommodate hutch; craft drill; 1^1/$_2$"l wood screws; white spray primer; white and green flat latex paint; paintbrushes; crackle medium; tracing paper; transfer paper; white, light green, green, dark green, light brown, brown, and dark brown acrylic paint; and natural sponges.

Refer to Painting Techniques, page 156, before beginning project. Allow primer, paint, and crackle medium to dry after each application unless otherwise indicated.

1. Follow *Preparing an Item for Painting*, page 156, to prepare hutch and table.
2. For cabinet, aligning back edges, position hutch on table. Using drill to make pilot holes and working from underneath table, use screws to attach hutch to table.
3. Apply primer to cabinet.
4. For crackled areas, use green latex paint to apply base coat to desired areas of cabinet. Follow manufacturer's instructions to apply crackle medium over

green paint. Use white latex paint to paint entire cabinet.
5. Follow *Making Patterns*, page 156, and trace flowerpot pattern, page 145, onto tracing paper. Use transfer paper to transfer flowerpot to inside back of cabinet. Paint flowerpot brown. Use sponge to add light brown highlights and dark brown shading. While paint is still wet, use sponge and brown paint to lightly

blend colors; allow to dry.
6. Sponge paint a green topiary ball between each shelf on inside back of cabinet. Use sponge to add white and light green highlights and dark green shading.
7. Connecting topiary balls to flowerpot, paint brown trunk. Paint stems extending from flowerpot. Sponge paint light green and green leaves over stems.

ON THE WILD SIDE

Take a walk on the wild side with this interesting game table that's also a great everyday accent piece. A painted chessboard tops an ordinary telephone table, and painted leopard spots give it stylish flair.

PAINTED CHESS TABLE

Recycled item: table with tabletop at least 14" x 15" and a drawer
You will also need items listed under *Preparing an Item for Painting* (page 156); white spray primer; beige, brown, and black acrylic paint; paintbrushes; stencil brush; gold liquid leaf; toothbrush; and clear acrylic spray sealer.

Refer to Painting Techniques, page 156, before beginning project. Allow primer, paint, and sealer to dry after each application.

1. Remove drawer from table and drawer pull from drawer. Follow *Preparing an Item for Painting*, page 156, to prepare table and drawer.
2. Apply primer to table and drawer. Painting tabletop beige, apply desired base coat color to remaining areas of table and drawer.
3. Paint designs on table sides, table legs, and drawer as desired (we painted leopard spots outlined in black on beige areas of table).
4. For checkerboard, lightly draw an 11" square at center of top of table. Divide 11" square into sixty-four 1³/₈" squares. Paint alternating squares black. Paint a ¹/₂"w border around checkerboard.

5. Use stencil brush to lightly apply gold leaf accents to black areas of table and drawer. Spatter paint table black.
6. Apply two to three coats of sealer to table.

7. Replace drawer pull on drawer, then drawer in table.

CHILD'S PLAY

CHILDREN'S GAME TABLE AND CHAIRS

Kids love games, and making this fun project is child's play! Affix a game board — they're easy to find at garage sales and flea markets — to a simple table that you build with pressed board and wooden legs. A pair of hand-painted chairs provides a place for two playmates to share in the fun.

Recycled items: children's game board and two child-size chairs

You will also need a handsaw, pressed board, white spray primer, four 21" table legs, masking tape, spray paint to coordinate with game board, assorted colors of acrylic paint, paintbrushes, tracing paper, compressed craft sponge, four table leg mounting brackets, wood-tone spray, matte acrylic spray sealer, and craft glue.

Refer to Painting Techniques, page 156, before beginning project. Allow primer, paint, wood-tone spray, sealer, and glue to dry after each application.

1. For tabletop, use handsaw to cut a piece of pressed board 4" larger on all sides than game board.

2. Apply primer to tabletop, table legs, and chairs. Use masking tape to mask off desired areas on tabletop (we masked off a 4" square in all corners and a 3"w border on all sides). Spray paint tabletop, table legs, and chairs.

3. Remove masking tape from tabletop. Using acrylic paints, paint corners, border, and edges of tabletop as desired (we painted the corners white with a 3$^{1}/_{2}$" dia. red circle, the border with 1"w black and white stripes, and the edges black with white dots).

4. For stars, trace small and large star patterns, page 153, onto tracing paper; cut out. Using patterns, cut stars from sponge. Sponge paint large stars on corners of tabletop, small stars on table legs, and large and small stars on chairs.

5. For table, using table leg mounting brackets and following manufacturer's instructions, attach table legs to tabletop.

6. Apply wood-tone spray, then two to three coats of sealer to table and chairs. Center and glue game board on table.

MIDNIGHT SNACK-LIGHT

Having trouble finding those midnight snacks? This fun and folksy kitchen lamp will help light the way! Recycled from two wooden canisters and a plastic mesh produce bag, this lamp is a necessity to avoid late-night bumps and bruises.

KITCHEN CANISTER LAMP

Recycled items: two wooden canisters with lids and a plastic mesh produce bag (we used a 10 lb grapefruit bag)
You will also need a craft drill, craft glue, lamp kit for bottle base, lampshade, rickrack, 18" of 1"w ribbon, and a ³/₄" dia. button.

Allow glue to dry after each application.

1. Drill a hole large enough to accommodate stopper of lamp kit through center of lid of smallest canister. Glue lids to canisters. Stack and glue canisters together.
2. Follow manufacturer's instructions to assemble lamp.
3. Measure height of lampshade from rim to rim. Measure around bottom rim of lampshade. Cut a piece from mesh bag the determined measurements. Gathering around top as necessary, wrap and glue edges of bag piece around edges of lampshade.
4. Trimming to fit, glue rickrack along top and bottom edge of lampshade. Tie ribbon into a bow. Glue bow to lampshade, then button to bow.

SOMETHING TO CROW ABOUT

*T*urn a novelty vase into a "de-light-ful" lamp. Cover the shade with a vintage tablecloth and add faux fruit and flowers, and this old rooster will have something to crow about!

CERAMIC VASE LAMP

Recycled items: decorative ceramic vase and a tablecloth

You will also need a lamp kit with a wooden base, assorted colors of acrylic paint, paintbrushes, artificial fruit picks, artificial flowers, hot glue gun, tissue paper, tape, spray adhesive, lampshade, and single-fold bias tape.

1. Paint base of lamp as desired; allow to dry.
2. Follow manufacturer's instructions to assemble lamp.
3. Arrange fruit picks and flowers in vase. Glue vase to base of lamp.
4. Follow *Covering a Lampshade*, page 158, to cover shade with tablecloth. Trimming to fit, inserting edges of lampshade into fold of bias tape, and overlappping ends at back, glue bias tape around top and bottom of lampshade.

THE NATURAL LOOK

Create the natural look of a garden patio on your doorstep (or anywhere around your home) with a hand-detailed rug. We created a brick design on an old braided floor mat using masking tape and spray paints; the leaves were applied with sponges.

PAINTED BRAIDED RUG

Recycled item: braided rug (we used a 19" x 20" rug)

You will also need white spray primer; ³/₄"w masking tape; peach, burgundy, grey, and black spray paint; tracing paper; compressed craft sponge; light green and green acrylic paint; and a paintbrush.

Refer to Painting Techniques, page 156, before beginning project. Allow primer and paint to dry after each application.

1. Apply primer to one side of rug.
2. Use masking tape to mask off brick pattern on rug. Spray paint rug black. Remove masking tape.
3. Lightly spray rug with peach, then burgundy, then grey paint.
4. For leaves, trace each leaf pattern, page 153, onto tracing paper; cut out. Using patterns, cut one small leaf and one large leaf from sponge. Sponge paint green leaves on rug. Use sponge to add light green highlights. Use paintbrush to paint vine between leaves on rug.

LET IT FLOW

*A*ssemble a unique
conversation piece for your
home with items you can find
at any junk shop! Our country
fountain really works, and it's
perfect for a lonely corner, the
porch, or kitchen. We salvaged
battered dishes and cutlery
and arranged them in an old
roasting pan for a "country
kitchen" look.

RUSTIC FOUNTAIN

Recycled items: roasting pan, rocks,
assorted dishes, and silverware
You will also need thread seal tape,
two 90° galvanized female elbows,
$1/2$" galvanized male hose bib, $1/2$" x 6"
galvanized pipe nipple, $1/2$" galvanized
male hose barb, craft drill, pump for a
small fountain, conduit strap, two $3/8$" dia.
bolts with nuts, and $1/2$" rubber tubing.

Use tape to seal each connection.

1. For fountain, use one elbow to connect
hose bib to pipe nipple. Use remaining
elbow to connect opposite end of pipe
nipple to hose barb.

2. Working on back side of fountain, use
craft drill to drill two $3/8$" dia. holes $13/4$"
apart $1/2$" from rim of pan. Place pump in
pan. Using conduit strap and bolts and
nuts, attach fountain and electrical cord
to side of pan; tighten bolts.
3. Trimming to fit, attach one end of
tubing to pump and opposite end to
hose barb.
4. Fill bottom of pan with rocks. Follow
pump manufacturer's recommendations
to fill pan with water.
5. Arrange dishes and silverware
over rocks.

SUITCASE SHOWCASE

Showcase your special treasures in a curio shelf made from an old suitcase! Romantic floral fabric and decorative welting are the keys to creating the Victorian look.

SUITCASE WALL SHELF

Recycled item: suitcase with hinged lid and a small key

You will also need items listed under *Preparing an Item for Painting* (page 156), white spray primer, ivory and gold acrylic paint, paintbrushes, $^1/_8$" dia. welting with lip, hot glue gun, craft knife, cutting mat, foam core board, fabric, spray adhesive, handsaw, $^1/_8$" x 6" x 36" and $^3/_{16}$" x 6" x 36" balsa wood planks, craft drill, two swivel hoop mirror hangers, decorative satin cord, and 24" of $^1/_8$"w ivory ribbon.

Allow primer and paint to dry after each application.

1. Take suitcase apart by removing screws from hinges in bottom of suitcase. Discard side of suitcase without handle.
2. Follow *Preparing an Item for Painting*, page 156, to prepare remaining side of suitcase.
3. Apply primer to outside of suitcase. Paint outside of suitcase ivory and trim and hardware gold.
4. Measure around inside edge of suitcase; add $^1/_2$". Cut a length of welting the determined measurement. Follow *Adding Welting*, page 159, to glue welting along inside edge of suitcase.
5. Measure width and height of inside back of suitcase. Use craft knife to cut a piece of foam core board the determined measurements. Cut a piece from fabric 1" larger on all sides than foam core board. Apply spray adhesive to wrong side of fabric. Smoothing edges to back, smooth fabric onto foam core board. Spot glue corners of fabric to secure. Glue fabric-covered foam core board in suitcase.
6. For inside top and bottom, measure width and depth of inside of suitcase. Use handsaw to cut two $^1/_8$" thick pieces of balsa wood the determined measurements. For each wood piece, cut one piece of fabric 1" larger on all sides. Apply spray adhesive to wrong side of fabric pieces. Smoothing edges to back, smooth fabric onto wood pieces. Spot glue corners of fabric to secure. Glue wood pieces to inside of suitcase.
7. Using measurements determined in Step 6, cut one each of $^1/_8$" thick and $^3/_{16}$" thick pieces of balsa wood. For shelf, glue pieces together. Cut a piece of fabric large enough to cover all sides of shelf. Apply spray adhesive to wrong side of fabric piece. Wrap fabric around shelf. Trim fabric even with ends of shelf.
8. For sides, measure height of inside of suitcase; subtract $^5/_{16}$". Measure depth of inside of suitcase. Use handsaw to cut two pieces of $^1/_8$" thick balsa wood the determined measurements. Cutting across width, cut each side piece in half. Cut a piece of fabric 1" larger on all sides than each side piece. Apply spray adhesive to wrong side of fabric pieces. Smoothing edges to back, smooth fabric onto wood pieces. Spot glue corners of fabric to secure.
9. Glue bottom side pieces in suitcase. Glue shelf to top of bottom side pieces and along back of suitcase. Glue remaining side pieces in suitcase.
10. Use drill to make pilot holes for hangers in back of suitcase. Attach hangers to suitcase.
11. Gluing ends to secure, wrap suitcase handle with cord. Use ribbon to attach key to handle.

CANDLE ART

*O*ld plastic dishes from the flea market become works of art when you combine them to make these decorative candle holders! The possibilities are endless — just stack and glue different pieces together, then paint and add cord trim to dress them up.

PLASTIC DISH CANDLESTICKS

Recycled items: assorted plastic dishes

You will also need silicone adhesive, beige spray paint, copper and gold acrylic paint, natural sponges, clear acrylic spray sealer, hot glue gun, and ¹/₄" dia. gold cord.

Refer to Painting Techniques, page 156, before beginning project. Allow adhesive, paint, and sealer to dry after each application.

1. For each candlestick, using silicone adhesive to glue dishes in place, stack dishes to form desired shape.
2. Spray paint candlestick beige. Sponge paint candlestick copper, then gold.
3. Apply two to three coats of sealer to candlestick.
4. Trimming to fit, hot glue cord around candlestick as desired.

TORTOISESHELL CLASSIC

*C*reate an elegant furniture accent from a timeworn piano bench! It's versatile enough to use anywhere — at the piano, in the hallway, or at the foot of a bed. You can create the tortoiseshell effect with a simple wood-staining technique.

TORTOISESHELL PIANO BENCH

Recycled item: piano bench

You will also need items listed under *Preparing an Item for Painting* (page 156); newspaper; gold spray paint; paintbrushes; and Minwax® Polyshades® oak, walnut, and mahogany gloss wood stains with varnish.

Allow paint to dry after each application. Use a clean paintbrush for each stain.

1. Follow *Preparing an Item for Painting*, page 156, to prepare bench.
2. Cover work area with newspaper.
3. Spray paint bench.
4. Allowing stain to drip from paintbrush, drop large drops of one stain randomly onto bench; do not stroke with paintbrush. While stain is still wet, drop large drops of second stain over first stain. Repeat with remaining stain to cover bench; allow to dry.

*P*ut a little bit of spring into the air with this beautiful butterfly chair. Transform an old wooden chair into a masterpiece by adorning it with painted motifs. Butterfly-motif fabric gives the pleated seat cushion a soft, light appearance.

YELLOW BUTTERFLY CHAIR

Recycled item: wooden ladder-back chair with removable seat

You will also need items listed under *Preparing an Item for Painting* (page 156), white spray primer, assorted colors of acrylic paint, paintbrushes, tracing paper, transfer paper, household sponge, clear acrylic spray sealer, black permanent medium-point marker, 2" thick foam pad, serrated knife, kraft paper, fabric, staple gun, and 1"w fusible web tape.

Refer to Painting Techniques, page 156, before beginning project. Allow primer, paint, and sealer to dry after each application.

1. Remove seat from chair. Follow *Preparing an Item for Painting*, page 156, to prepare chair.
2. Apply primer to chair. Paint desired base coat on chair (we used a darker color to add shading).
3. Trace leaves, vine, and butterfly design, page 146, onto tracing paper. Use transfer paper to transfer design to top rung of chair. Paint design. Paint flowers and vines on uprights. Using desired color paint, lightly sponge paint over designs.
4. Apply two or three coats of sealer to chair.
5. For seat, use marker to draw around seat on foam pad. Use knife to cut foam pad along drawn lines.
6. For seat cover pattern, draw around seat on kraft paper. Cut kraft paper 6" outside drawn line. Use pattern to cut fabric for seat cover.
7. Place fabric wrong side up on flat surface. Center foam pad, then seat on fabric. Fold corners of fabric diagonally

over corners of seat; staple to secure. Fold edges of fabric over edges of seat; staple to secure.
8. For skirt front, measure along top edge of seat front; add 5¹/₂". Cut a piece from fabric 6¹/₄"w by the determined measurement. For each side skirt, measure along top edge of side of seat; add 3¹/₄". Cut a piece from fabric 6¹/₄"w by the determined measurement. Press edges of each skirt piece ¹/₄" to wrong side twice; stitch in place.
9. Press two ¹/₂" pleats 3¹/₂" from each side of skirt front (Fig. 1). Following manufacturer's instructions, use ¹/₂" lengths of web tape to fuse top edges of each pleat together (Fig. 2).

Fig. 1

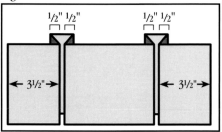

Fig. 2

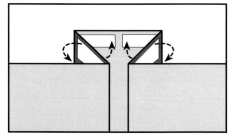

10. For each side skirt, press two ¹/₂" pleats at center of each side skirt piece. Use ¹/₂" lengths of web tape to fuse top edges of each pleat together.
11. Staple top edge of each skirt piece along edge of seat. Replace seat.

"SEW" LOVELY

A leafy green friend will look "sew" lovely spilling over the sides of this delicately painted planter. Transform an old knitting or sewing basket into a plant stand by stenciling pastel flowers around the outside.

PLANTER

Recycled item: old-fashioned knitting stand

You will also need items listed under *Preparing an Item for Painting* (page 156); masking tape; white spray primer; peach and green spray paint; sandpaper; light pink, pink, light green, and green acrylic paint; paintbrushes; stencil plastic; craft knife; cutting mat; stencil brushes; and clear acrylic spray sealer.

Allow primer, paint, and sealer to dry after each application.

1. Follow *Preparing an Item for Painting*, page 156, to prepare stand. If necessary, mask decorative trim on stand.
2. Apply primer to stand. Spray paint stand green, then peach. Lightly sand stand to expose small patches of green. Paint stripes on legs as desired.
3. Use tulip pattern, page 152, and follow *Stenciling*, page 157, to stencil tulips around stand.
4. Apply two to three coats of sealer to stand.

COUNTRY GARDEN LAMP

*A*dd a touch of old-fashioned country to your kitchen with a crafty water pump lamp. A lamp kit changes a flea market find into a one-of-a-kind base. Cover the shade with brown paper, then decoupage with seed packets and add fabric trim.

WATER PUMP LAMP

Recycled items: hand-pump water pump, brown paper bags, and seed packets
You will also need a hacksaw, ¹/₈" dia. I.P. pipe stem, spray paint to match water pump, lamp kit, lampshade, craft glue, foam brush, decorative-edge craft scissors, black permanent medium-point marker, and fabric for lampshade trim.

1. Measure height of pump. Use hacksaw to cut a length of pipe stem the determined measurement. Spray paint pipe stem; allow to dry.
2. For lamp, loosen tension bolts. Remove plunger and lid from pump.
3. Thread pipe through center of pump. Replace lid, then plunger on pump; tighten tension bolts.
4. Threading cord of lamp kit through pipe from bottom of pump, follow manufacturer's instructions to assemble lamp.
5. For lampshade, tear pieces from paper bags. Mix one part glue with one part water. Use foam brush to apply glue mixture to back of paper bag pieces. Covering lampshade, smooth paper bag pieces onto lampshade; allow to dry.
6. For each motif, use craft scissors to cut front from seed packet. Use foam brush to apply glue mixture to wrong side of motif. Arrange and smooth motifs onto

lampshade; allow to dry. Use marker to draw "stitches" around each motif.
7. Measure around top and bottom of lampshade; add ¹/₂" to each measurement.

Use craft scissors to cut one 1"w fabric strip by each determined measurement. Glue strips around top and bottom of lampshade; allow to dry.

ROOSTER CABINET

Recycled item: cabinet with front panels

Cock-a doodle-doo! It's so easy to turn a weathered cabinet into a haven for roosters. Cut these fine feathered chanticleers from print fabric, glue onto the front panel of the cabinet, and then cover with chicken wire.

You will also need items listed under *Preparing an Item for Painting* (page 156); white spray primer; green and brown flat latex paint; paintbrushes; crackle medium; gold, red, green, tan, and brown acrylic paint; fusible fabric stabilizer; rooster-motif fabric; craft glue; wire cutters; 1" poultry netting; staple gun; handsaw; 3/4"w screen moulding; craft drill; 1/2"l wood nails; 1 3/4" wooden egg; wood-tone spray; and leather lacing.

Refer to Painting Techniques, page 156, before beginning project. Allow primer, paint, crackle medium, glue, and wood-tone spray to dry after each application unless otherwise indicated.

1. Remove knob or handle from cabinet. Follow *Preparing an Item for Painting*, page 156, to prepare cabinet.
2. Apply primer to cabinet.
3. Working with wood grain and leaving front panels unpainted, apply a brown latex base coat on cabinet. Follow manufacturer's instructions to apply crackle medium over base coat. Use green latex paint to paint over crackle medium.

4. Use dry paintbrush to paint front panels tan. Use dry paintbrush and brown paint to add wood grain and weathered details to panels. Paint a brown "perch" for each rooster. Paint gold "straw" on each "perch." While paint is still wet, add brown shading to "straw."
5. Fuse stabilizer to back of fabric. Carefully cut roosters from fabric. Arrange and glue roosters to front panels.
6. Measure width and height of each front panel; add 1/2" to each measurement. Use wire cutters to cut a piece of poultry netting for each panel the determined measurements. Staple poultry netting over front panels.
7. Measure width of each panel; add 1 1/2". Use handsaw to cut a piece of moulding for top and bottom of each panel the determined measurement. Measure length of each panel. Use handsaw to cut a piece of moulding for each side the determined measurement. Use craft drill to make pilot holes in ends of each moulding piece.
8. Using acrylic paint, paint green and gold "check" pattern on each moulding piece. Add red details to each gold "check."
9. Use nails to attach side, then top and bottom moulding pieces around each front panel, covering edges of poultry netting.
10. For knob, paint wooden egg tan. Lightly apply wood-tone spray to egg. Use craft drill to make pilot hole in center of egg. Using hardware from original knob, attach knob to cabinet door.
11. Use craft drill to drill a 1/4" dia. hole in cabinet opposite knob. Thread ends of lacing through hole; leaving a loop large enough to fit over knob, knot ends together on inside of cabinet.

FAVORITE THINGS

*Y*ou can revive a wicker
storage bench to create a handsome
hideaway for your favorite things.
Spray paint the bench and choose
coordinating fabrics, and you've
got a keepsake!

FABRIC-COVERED BENCH

Recycled item: cardboard and a wicker
bench with handles and removable lid
You will also need white spray paint,
fabric, batting, staple gun, hot glue gun,
spray adhesive, 3/8" dia. welting with lip,
handsaw, and 1" dia. wooden dowels.

1. Remove lid from bench. Spray paint
bench white; allow to dry.
2. For lid, cut one piece each of fabric
and batting 2" larger on all sides than lid.
Place fabric wrong side up on flat surface.
Center batting, then lid on fabric. Fold
corners of fabric diagonally over corners
of lid; staple to secure. Fold edges of
fabric over edges of lid; staple to secure.
3. For lid loop, cut a 1½" x 11" piece of
fabric. Press each long edge 3/8" to wrong
side. Crossing ends of loop, center and
glue ends to wrong side of lid.
4. Cut a piece of cardboard ½" smaller
on all sides than lid. Cut a piece of fabric
1" larger on all sides than cardboard.
Apply spray adhesive to wrong side of
fabric piece. Smoothing edges to back,
smooth fabric onto cardboard. Spot glue
corners of fabric to secure. Covering lid
loop, glue fabric-covered cardboard to
inside of lid.
5. For each bench handle, measure length
and circumference of handle. Cut a piece
of batting the determined measurements.
Cut a piece of fabric ½" larger on all

sides than batting. Press edges of fabric
½" to wrong side. Wrap batting around
handle; glue to secure. With edges of
fabric overlapping on underside of
handle, wrap fabric around handle; glue
to secure.
6. Measure around opening in bench; add
1". Cut a length from welting the
determined measurement. Overlapping at
back, staple lip of welting along inside
edge of bench.
7. Measure length of each opening edge.
Use handsaw to cut one length from
dowels for each measurement. For each

fabric-covered dowel, cut a piece of
batting 3½" by the determined length. Cut
a piece of fabric ½" larger on all sides
than batting. Press edges of fabric ½" to
wrong side. Wrap batting around dowel;
glue to secure. With edges of fabric
overlapping on underside of dowel, wrap
dowel with fabric; glue to secure. Glue
fabric-covered dowels to opening edges
of bench.
8. Glue a piece of batting around each
foot. Gathering fabric at top, wrap a piece
of fabric around foot. Glue gathers to foot
to secure.

"THROWAWAY" WASTEBASKET

*T*oss *your trash into a container that was once a throwaway itself! Cover an old metal waste can with intricate fabrics and add a decorative emblem. We chose a crown medallion to give it manly appeal.*

FABRIC-COVERED WASTEBASKET

Recycled item: metal wastebasket
You will also need three coordinating fabrics, hot glue gun, $1/2$"w gimp trim, $1/4$" dia. decorative cord, wire cutters, four gold thumb tacks, and a charm.

1. Measure around wastebasket; add 1". Measure height of wastebasket between rims. Cut a piece from one fabric the determined measurements. Overlapping ends at back, glue fabric around wastebasket.
2. For panel, measure height of wastebasket between rims. Cut a piece from second fabric $6^{1}/4$"w by the determined measurement. Position and glue fabric to wastebasket. Trimming to fit, glue a length of trim to each long edge of panel.
3. Cut a $4^{7}/8$" square from third fabric. Position and glue fabric square to panel. Trimming to fit, glue cord around square and top and bottom of wastebasket. Use wire cutters to cut heads from tacks. Glue tack heads to cord at corners of fabric square. Center and glue charm to fabric square.

ALL THROUGH THE HOUSE

From the kitchen to the bedroom, spruce up your house with these fun decorative crafts! In this section, you'll discover treasures to create from old relics that may be scattered throughout your home. Put your feet up and relax surrounded by the homespun warmth of our daisy lamp or candles displayed in golden holders. Small juice bottles become lovely vases, egg carton cutouts transform into a beautiful posy topiary, and a timeworn chair is given new life. Each and every room will be filled with masterpieces that have been enhanced with your clever creativity!

PUT YOUR FEET UP!

*P*ut your feet up and relax!
Choose your favorite fabric to
cover a battered ottoman, and
create an elegant pouf using
the lid of a snack chip container.
Simply glue on buttons and hang
tassels for a fabulous finish!

FABRIC-COVERED OTTOMAN

Recycled items: square ottoman and a
plastic lid from snack chip container

You will also need batting, fabric, staple
gun, heavy-duty thread, purchased pillow
large enough to cover top of ottoman, hot
glue gun, nine 1" dia. buttons, and four
beaded tassels.

1. If necessary, remove feet or legs from
ottoman; discard.
2. Measure from bottom edge on one side
of ottoman to opposite bottom edge; add
6" (Fig. 1). Cut three squares of batting
and one square of fabric the determined
measurement.

Fig. 1

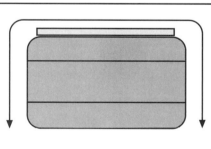

3. Center one piece of batting over top of
ottoman. Pulling batting taut and
gathering excess at corners, use staple
gun to staple edges of batting to underside
of ottoman. Repeat for remaining batting
pieces and fabric.

4. For pillow accent, thread needle with
heavy-duty thread. Leaving a 5" tail and
working from back of pillow, insert
needle through center of pillow, then
plastic lid. Insert needle $1/4$" away, back
through lid, then pillow. Tie thread ends
tightly at back of pillow to secure. Cut a
10" square of fabric. Center fabric square
over lid. Loosely tuck fabric edges under
lid; glue to secure. Glue one button to
center of pillow accent.
5. Place pillow on top of ottoman. Staple
corners and center of each side edge of
pillow to ottoman. Glue one tassel to each
corner. Glue buttons to corners and at
center of each side edge of pillow,
covering staples.

KEEPIN' COWBOY TIME

*K*ids *will get a kick out of keeping time with this Western-style clock! A child's outgrown footwear is transformed by fitting a clock face into one side of the boot. Add a lariat, bandanna, and toy badge to make it a real cowpoke timekeeper.*

BOOT CLOCK

Recycled item: cowboy boot
You will also need a drawing compass, craft knife, 2⁵⁄₈" dia. bezel clock movement, hot glue gun, bandanna, 2¹⁄₄ yds. of rope, and a plastic sheriff badge.

1. Using compass, center and draw a 2³⁄₈" dia. circle on one side of boot.
2. Use craft knife to cut ¹⁄₄" inside drawn circle. Cut slits at ¹⁄₄" intervals to drawn line.
3. Insert clock movement into hole in boot; glue to secure.
4. Arrange bandanna, rope, and badge in boot.

REFURBISHED WITH STYLE

*F*urniture fix-ups are fun, and this project is no exception! Refurbish that old, dusty end table with a fresh coat of paint and stylish stenciled designs. The newly gilded table will be an elegant accent for any home.

STYLISH ACCENT TABLE

Recycled item: accent table

You will also need items listed under *Preparing an Item for Painting* (page 156), grey spray primer, black latex paint, paintbrushes, gold acrylic paint, stencil plastic, craft knife, cutting mat, and a stencil brush.

Allow primer and paint to dry after each application.

1. Follow *Preparing an Item for Painting*, page 156, to prepare table.
2. Apply primer to table. Paint table black. Paint gold accents on legs and edges of table.
3. Use pattern, page 143, and follow *Stenciling*, page 157, to stencil gold leaves on table.

DAISY DAZZLE

*E*nergize your favorite reading corner with our eye-catching lampshade. You simply wrap ribbon around a "recycled" wire frame and add rickrack and daisy-motif trim. What an inventive way to add dazzle to an ordinary lamp!

RIBBON LAMPSHADE

Recycled item: lampshade frame

You will also need craft glue, 1½"w ribbon, jumbo rickrack, and daisy-motif trim.

Allow glue to dry after each application.

1. Glue one end of ribbon to top of frame. Pulling ribbon taut and overlapping as necessary to cover frame, bring ribbon down over bottom of frame and up through inside of frame. Continue wrapping ribbon around frame. Glue remaining end of ribbon to frame to secure.
2. Trimming to fit, glue rickrack around top and bottom of frame.
3. Cut daisy motifs from trim. Glue motifs to rickrack on frame.

HOMESPUN INSPIRATIONS

VINTAGE LINEN PILLOWS

Preserve pieces of the past with a pair of homespun pillows sewn using the best sections from worn quilts, bedspreads, and vintage linens. For inspiration, look no further than your own linen closet!

Match right sides and raw edges and use a 1/4" seam allowance for all sewing unless otherwise indicated.

ENVELOPE PILLOW

Recycled items: tablecloth with a decorative corner, quilt, and a 1" dia. button
You will also need fabric, straight pin, 31" of decorative trim, and polyester fiberfill.

1. For flap front and back, cut a 16" square from decorative corner of tablecloth. Leaving decorative area uncut, cut square in half diagonally.
2. For ruffle, cut a 6" x 64" strip, piecing as necessary, from fabric. Matching long edges, sew across each end of strip. Turn right side out; press. Baste along long raw edges. Use pin to mark ruffle 32" from one end. Pull basting threads to gather ruffle to measure 30".
3. Aligning pin in ruffle with point of flap front, baste ruffle to adjacent edges of right side of flap front. Leaving long edges open for turning, sew flap back to flap front; clip at point. Turn flap right side out; press.
4. Press each end of trim 1/2" to wrong side. Sew trim along edge of flap front.
5. For pillow front and back, cut two 22" squares from quilt. Baste flap to pillow back. Being careful not to catch ruffle in seam allowance and leaving an opening for turning, sew pillow front and pillow back together. Clip corners; turn right side out. Stuff pillow with fiberfill; sew opening closed. Use button to sew flap to pillow front at point of flap.

LAYERED PILLOW

Recycled items: assorted vintage linens (we used handkerchiefs, kitchen towels, and doilies) and a bedspread
You will also need fabric, straight pin, decorative trim, pom-pom fringe, and polyester fiberfill.

1. For pillow front, cut a 12" x 15³/₄" piece from fabric. Center and layer linens on pillow front. Cut a decorative 6¹/₄" x 8" piece from towel. Center towel piece on layered linens; pin to secure. Sewing through all layers, sew towel piece to pillow front. Sew trim along edges of towel piece.
2. Cut two 3¹/₂" x 23" top/bottom borders, two 3¹/₂" x 13" side borders, and one 19" x 23" pillow back from bedspread. Sew side, then top/bottom borders to pillow front. Trimming to fit and mitering corners, sew fringe along inside edges of borders.
3. Leaving an opening for turning, sew pillow front and pillow back together. Clip corners; turn right side out.
4. Leaving a 2"w opening on same side as opening for turning, sew along inside edge of borders (Fig. 1). Stuff pillow with fiberfill. Sew both openings closed.

Fig. 1

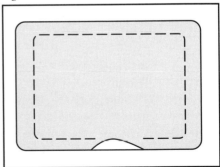

GARDEN BEAUTIES

Weathered frames and pressed greenery capture the beauty of the garden. Simply glue the greenery to card stock and insert it into whitewashed frames. These simple projects are a wonderful way to make use of old frames and to decorate your home with the essence of nature.

FRAMED BOTANICALS

Recycled items: frames

You will also need fine-grit sandpaper, tack cloth, white and brown acrylic paint, paintbrushes, paste floor wax, craft knife, cutting mat, mat board, craft glue, dried greenery (we used Boston Fern and Plumosa), black calligraphy pen, matte acrylic spray sealer, and glass to fit in frame.

1. For each frame, painting a brown base coat on frame, follow *Weathered Whitewash Technique*, page 157, to paint frame.
2. Use craft knife to cut a piece of mat board to fit frame. Glue greenery to mat board; allow to dry. Use pen to write name of greenery on mat board. Lightly apply sealer over greenery; allow to dry.
3. Mount mat board in frame under glass.

GOOD "SCENTS"

*D*on't throw out those plain wire hangers when it makes good "scents" to use them to create pretty closet sachets like this one! A tissue paper-covered plastic bag is simply filled with potpourri and affixed to a hanger.

CLOSET POTPOURRI HANGER

Recycled item: wire hanger

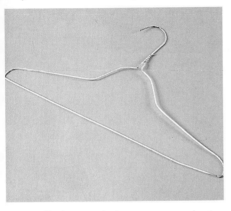

You will also need wire cutters, push pin, resealable plastic bag, potpourri, decorative gold tissue paper, transparent tape, craft glue, and 17" of 1½"w sheer gold ribbon.

Allow glue to dry after each application.

1. Using wire cutters and leaving 3" on each side of hook, cut hook from hanger; discard remainder of hanger. Straighten wire at each side of hook to 90°.
2. Use push pin to make several holes in plastic bag. Fill plastic bag with potpourri; seal bag.
3. Cut an 8" x 19" piece of tissue paper. Fold each long edge 1" to wrong side; tape to secure. Matching short ends, fold paper in half; unfold. Tape potpourri bag to wrong side of paper just above fold.

Refold paper; glue edges to secure.
4. For flap, fold glued edges 1½" to back; unfold. Cut center of flap from edge to fold. Position base of hook along fold. Fold flap over wire; glue to secure.
5. Tie ribbon into a bow around hanger.

PAINTED PIZZAZZ

*A*dd *pizzazz to a cozy nook with this charming chair! Warm hues and simple painted designs convert a plain wooden chair into a showpiece. For a refreshing finish, choose a coordinating fabric to cover the seat.*

PAINTED CHAIR

Recycled item: wooden chair with removable seat

You will also need items listed under *Preparing an Item for Painting* (page 156), white spray primer, assorted colors of acrylic paint, assorted paintbrushes, matte acrylic spray sealer, kraft paper, batting, fabric to cover seat, and a staple gun.

Allow primer, paint, and sealer to dry after each application.

1. Remove seat from chair.
2. Follow *Preparing an Item for Painting*, page 156, to prepare chair.
3. Apply primer to chair. Paint desired color base coats on chair (we painted sections of the legs and uprights alternating colors).
4. Paint designs on chair (we painted flowers, leaves, dots, and teardrops).

5. Apply two to three coats of sealer to chair.
6. For seat cover pattern, draw around seat on kraft paper. Cut kraft paper 3" outside drawn line. Using pattern, cut several pieces from batting. Cut one piece of fabric 3" outside edges of pattern.

7. Place fabric wrong side up on flat surface. Center batting pieces, then seat on fabric. Fold corners of fabric diagonally over corners of seat; staple to secure. Fold edges of fabric over edges of seat; staple to secure. Replace seat.

112

BREAKFAST IN BED

*S*tart the day off right with breakfast in bed! Painted in pretty pastels, this beautiful tray lightens up the morning. When you're not using it, you'll want to leave it out as a stylish accent.

CRACKLED BREAKFAST TRAY

Recycled item: wooden lap tray

You will also need white spray primer; light yellow, yellow, peach, and green acrylic paint; paintbrushes; and crackle medium.

Allow primer, paint, and crackle medium to dry after each application.

1. Apply primer to tray.
2. Paint tray peach. Follow manufacturer's instructions to apply crackle medium over peach paint. Paint tray green.
3. Using light yellow and yellow paint, paint details on tray as desired.

SHOE BOX SUITCASE

Recycled item: shoe box and scraps of wallpaper

Fig. 1

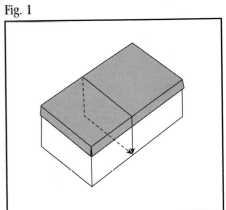

You will also need a ruler, spray adhesive, craft knife, cutting mat, 1"w grosgrain ribbon, sewing thread in a contrasting color, hot glue gun, two 1" D-rings, two 1" square hook and loop fasteners, two $1^3/_8$"w buckles, wire cutters, and four gold thumb tacks.

Every seasoned traveler needs a handy place to stow his or her getaway gear! To transform a plain shoe box into a clever keeper, simply cover with wallpaper and ribbon. This little "suitcase" can be used to store traveling items such as tickets, passports, and visas while you're preparing for a trip.

1. Remove lid from box. For suitcase, follow *Covering a Box*, page 159, to cover box and lid with paper.
2. For suitcase trim, measure around lid; add $^1/_2$". Measure around bottom of box; add $^1/_2$". Cut one length of ribbon for each determined measurement. Topstitch along edges of each of ribbon. Overlapping ends at back, glue trim around lid and bottom of suitcase.
3. Place lid on box. Beginning and ending at bottom edge of box front, measure around box; add 2" (Fig. 1). Cut one length of ribbon for each closure strap the determined measurement. Cut one 7" length of ribbon for handle. Topstitch along edges of each ribbon.

4. For handle, wrap 1" of each end of handle around flat edge of one D-ring; glue to secure. Spacing rings $3^1/_2$" apart, glue D-rings to front of suitcase.
5. For each closure strap, glue hook side of fastener to right side of one end of strap. Fold opposite end 1" to wrong side; glue to secure. Glue loop side of fastener to wrong side of folded end.
6. Thread one buckle onto each strap. Placing one closure strap at each side of handle, wrap strap around box with hook and loop fasteners joining over bottom trim of suitcase. Position and glue buckle on lid to secure. Leaving portion of closure strap between lid and front of box unglued, glue closure strap around suitcase.
7. Use wire cutters to cut heads from tacks. Glue tack heads to closure straps on suitcase front.

HOMEY BRAIDED COASTERS

*A*re your plastic grocery
bags piling up? Put them to use by
crafting these decorative coasters!
Fashioned from colorful bags, a
small plastic produce container,
and a cast-off piece of costume
jewelry, this set will add a homey
touch to the den.

BRAIDED COASTERS

Recycled items: plastic grocery bags,
pint-size open-mesh plastic produce
container, and a pin

You will also need a low-temperature
glue gun and 3⁷/₈" dia. cork coasters.

1. For each coaster, cut three 3" x 37"
strips from plastic bags. Glue strips
together at one end. Braid strips
together. Glue remaining ends together to secure.
Beginning at center, coil and glue braided
strip on coaster.

2. Measure around produce container;
add ¹/₂". Cut three 2"w strips from plastic
bags the determined measurement.
Matching long edges, fold strips in half.
Beginning and ending at back, weave
strips through sides of container; spot
glue to secure.

3. Cut one 2¹/₂" x 10" strip from plastic
bag. Tie strip into a bow. Glue bow to
container; glue pin to knot of bow.

TRENDY PHOTO TREE

*D*on't spend a fortune on a
gift-shop picture frame — make
this unique photo holder using
things that would ordinarily be
thrown away! It's a cinch to insert
lengths of wire coat hangers into
stacked wooden spools. Layers of
sponge painting create an antique
look for the base.

WIRE PHOTO HOLDER

Recycled items: wire coat hangers
You will also need a hot glue gun; three
wooden spools; 2³/₄" square wooden
corner moulding; wire cutters; pliers;
electrical tape; gold spray paint; glazing
medium; copper, brown, and black
acrylic paint; natural sponges; and clear
acrylic spray sealer.

*Refer to Painting Techniques, page 156,
before beginning project. Allow paint
and sealer to dry after each application.*

1. For base, stack and glue spools to
moulding.
2. For anchor holder, measure base from
top of moulding to top of base; add 14".
Use wire cutters to cut one length from
hanger the determined measurement. Cut
one 11¹/₂", one 10¹/₂", and two 12"
lengths from hangers.
3. Insert anchor holder into base.
Mark anchor holder at top of base;
remove wire.
4. Leaving end of anchor holder below
mark and 1" of remaining wires straight,
use pliers to shape holders and to bend
opposite end of each wire into a spiral.

5. Use tape to attach straight ends of
holders around anchor holder at mark.
Apply glue to straight end of anchor
holder. Insert into base.
6. Spray paint holder gold.

7. For each acrylic paint color, mix one
part glazing medium with one part paint.
Sponge paint base brown, then copper,
then black. Apply two to three coats of
sealer to holder.

You'll receive glowing compliments when you display these decorative candle holders. The golden accents are a snap to make using salvaged window screen, glass jars, and cardboard.

SCREEN CANDLE HOLDERS

Recycled items: window screen, pint-size glass jars for large candle holders, and cardboard

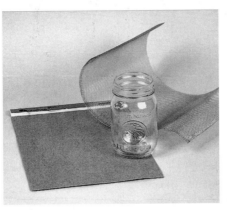

You will also need heavy gloves, wire cutters, gold spray paint, clear glass votive cups for small candle holders, fine-gauge craft wire, tracing paper, and a push pin.

1. Wearing gloves, use wire cutters to cut a 15" square from screen for each large candle holder or a 9" square from screen for each small candle holder. Fold edges of each screen piece ¼" to wrong side.
2. Spray paint screen pieces; allow to dry.
3. Center jar or votive cup on screen piece. Pleating evenly, gather screen piece around jar or votive cup. Weave wire through holes in pleats of screen around jar or cup; twist ends together to secure.
4. Using large star pattern, page 143, for large candle holder or small star pattern, page 143, for small candle holder, trace pattern onto tracing paper; cut out. Using pattern, cut four stars for each candle holder from cardboard.
5. Spray paint both sides of each star; allow to dry.
6. Use push pin to make one hole in one point of each star. Use wire to attach stars to points of candle holders.

FRUGAL GOURMET

*H*ere's a novel idea for any "frugal gourmet" — turn a small detergent box and grocery ads into a handy coupon organizer. A miniature rolling-pin handle adds the final touch to this charming shopper's companion.

COUPON HOLDER

Recycled items: grocery advertisements from newspapers and a small detergent box

You will also need craft glue, foam brush, white and red acrylic paint, paintbrushes, 5"l craft rolling pin, red permanent medium-point marker, push pin, two 6" lengths of medium-gauge craft wire, felt, and a hot glue gun.

Allow paint to dry after each application.

1. Cut desired motifs from grocery advertisements. Mix one part craft glue with one part water. Use foam brush to apply glue mixture to wrong side of motifs. Entirely covering outside of box and lid and folding to the inside as necessary, position and smooth motifs onto detergent box. Apply glue mixture over box; allow to dry.

2. Paint rolling pin white; paint handles red. Use marker to write "Coupons" on rolling pin.

3. Use push pin to make two pilot holes 4" apart in center of lid. Wrap one end of each length of wire around each handle. Thread remaining end of each length of wire through pilot hole in lid; twist wire ends together to secure.

4. Measure width and length of inside of lid. Cut a piece of felt the determined measurements. Hot glue felt piece inside lid covering wire.

MAGNETIC ART

*C*reate magnetic art for your
kitchen or gardening shed! It's easy
to cut motifs from old calendars,
then add buttons and ribbons.

CALENDAR MAGNETS

Recycled items: calendars

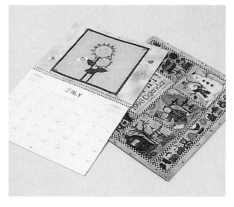

You will also need a hot glue gun, items
to assemble and decorate magnets (we
used card stock, decorative paper,
decorative-edge craft scissors, ribbon,
corrugated cardboard, and buttons), and
³/₄" dia. magnets.

1. For cut-out magnet, cut desired motif
from calendar. Glue motif to card stock;
cut out along edges of motif. Glue magnet
to back of motif.
2. For hanging magnet, cut two desired
motifs from calendar. Glue one motif to
decorative paper. Use craft scissors to
trim paper ¹/₄" from motif. Glue paper to
card stock. Trim card stock to ¹/₈" from
paper. Glue ends of ribbon to back of
card stock. Glue second motif to ribbon.
Glue magnet to back of second motif.

3. For button magnet, cut desired motif
from calendar. Glue motif to corrugated
cardboard. Use craft scissors to trim
cardboard to ¹/₂" from motif. Glue
buttons to motif. Glue magnet to back
of cardboard.

ON PINS AND NEEDLES

*R*ound up an empty tape roll and you're on your way to making a fanciful pincushion for your sewing basket. The no-sew project also utilizes bits from your collection of scrap fabrics and buttons.

TAPE ROLL PINCUSHION

Recycled items: 2¹/₄" h x 3¹/₄" dia. cardboard tape roll, lightweight cardboard, 12" of 2mm silk ribbon, one ³/₄" dia. button, and four ¹/₂" dia. buttons

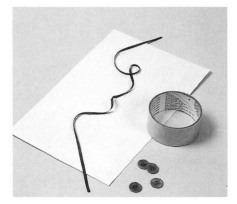

You will also need a push pin, fabric, hot glue gun, spray adhesive, polyester fiberfill, 2" x 10³/₄" piece of batting, 11" of ³/₈"w grosgrain ribbon, decorative satin cord, white string pearls, 11¹/₄" of 2¹/₄"w ribbon, and a soft sculpture needle.

1. Draw around tape roll on cardboard. Cut out circle along drawn lines. Use push pin to punch hole in center of cardboard circle. Leaving at least 1" between shapes, draw around tape roll twice on wrong side of fabric. Cut out circles ¹/₂" outside drawn line.
2. For pincushion, gathering to fit, glue edge of one fabric circle along one open

edge of tape roll. Apply spray adhesive to wrong side of remaining fabric circle. Center and smooth fabric onto cardboard circle. Clipping as necessary, smooth edges of fabric over to back of cardboard circle.
3. Stuff pincushion with fiberfill. Glue fabric-covered cardboard circle to remaining open edge of pincushion.
4. Glue batting around outside of pincushion. Overlapping as necessary, glue grosgrain ribbon around bottom edge of pincushion.
5. Trimming to fit, glue cord, then pearls around top edge of pincushion.
6. Press one end of 2¹/₄"w ribbon ¹/₄" to wrong side. Glue ribbon around outside of pincushion. Trimming to fit, glue pearls around outside of pincushion.

7. Thread needle with silk ribbon. Leaving a 3" tail of silk ribbon at top, insert needle through ³/₄" dia. button, through top of pincushion to hole in bottom of pincushion; bring needle back up through pincushion, then button (Fig. 1). Tie ribbon ends into a bow; knot ends.

Fig. 1

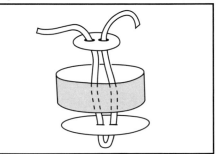

8. For "feet," glue ¹/₂" dia. buttons to bottom of pincushion.

DARLING DOLL

*B*ring old-fashioned charm
to a bedroom or sitting room with
this darling doll. Flea markets and
garage sales provide linens aplenty,
so finding the perfect towel for your
project is a snap! Curly hair and
a doily bonnet frame her simple
hand-drawn face.

TEA TOWEL DOLL

Recycled item: embroidered tea towel
You will also need tracing paper,
embroidery floss, 11"h cloth doll body,
black permanent fine-point marker,
cosmetic blush, hot glue gun, curly doll
hair, 5" dia. white doily, and two 9"
lengths of ¹/₄"w grosgrain ribbon.

1. Use pattern, page 151, and follow
Making Patterns, page 156, to make
bodice pattern.
2. Matching short ends, fold towel in half.
Aligning shoulders with fold, cut bodice
from towel. Cut out neck opening. Using
hemmed edge as one 12" side of
rectangle, cut two 10¹/₂" x 12" pieces
from towel for skirt.
3. Matching right sides and using a ¹/₄"
seam allowance, sew along sleeves and
sides of bodice. Clipping as necessary,
press neck opening and each sleeve edge
¹/₈" to wrong side; sew in place. Turn
bodice right side out. Leaving a 4" tail at
each end, use three strands of floss to
work *Running Stitches*, page 158, ³/₄"
from each sleeve edge. Place bodice on
doll. Pull floss ends to gather sleeves
around each arm. Tie floss ends into
a bow.

4. Matching right sides and hems, use a
¹/₄" seam allowance to sew sides of skirt
together. Turn skirt right side out. For
waist, press unhemmed edge ¹/₄" to
wrong side. Beginning and ending at
center front and leaving a 6" tail at each
end, use three strands of floss to work
Running Stitches along pressed edge.
Place skirt on doll. Pull floss ends to
gather skirt around waist. Tie floss ends
into a bow.

5. Use marker to make dots for eyes.
Apply blush for cheeks. Glue doll hair
to head.
6. For bonnet, use three strands of floss
to work *Running Stitches* across doily
1¹/₂" from one edge. Gather doily slightly;
knot floss at each end to secure. Tack one
end of each ribbon length at each side of
gathered edge. Position and tack bonnet
onto back of head. Tie ribbon ends into a
bow around neck.

TREASURE BOX

Treasure chests bring with them a spirit of adventure. A perfect hiding place for your "riches," this little chest has a unique look. To create the clever box, we used an empty salt container and a small cardboard box. The intriguing texture is achieved by crumpling tissue paper, gluing it to the box, and then painting.

Recycled items: 3¹/₂" dia. x 5¹/₂"h salt container and a 1³/₈" x 3¹/₂" x 5¹/₂" cardboard box

You will also need a craft knife, hot glue gun, tissue paper, craft glue, red and gold acrylic paint, paintbrush, household sponge, gold fringe, and red card stock.

Refer to Painting Techniques, page 156, before beginning project. Allow glue and paint to dry after each application. Use hot glue for all gluing unless otherwise indicated.

1. For lid, use craft knife to cut salt container in half lengthwise; discard one half.
2. For bottom of box, glue open flaps together to reseal box. Use craft knife to cut along two short and one long edge of box front. For hinge, trim box front to 1". Glue hinge inside lid.
3. For stability, cut a 3¹/₂" x 5¹/₂" piece of card stock. Glue card stock piece to bottom of box.
4. Lightly crumple tissue paper; smooth out. Trimming to fit, cut a piece of tissue paper large enough to cover lid. Trimming to fit, cut a piece of tissue paper large enough to cover bottom of box. Use craft glue to glue tissue paper to outside of box.
5. Paint box red, then sponge paint gold.
6. Measure around edge of lid; add ¹/₂". Cut a length of fringe the determined measurement. Overlapping ends at back, glue fringe around lid.

BOTTLE BUNCH

*D*on't toss those seemingly
useless juice bottles — use them
to create a pretty clustered vase.
Simply spray paint the containers
and add basic flower designs. Tie
ribbon around the cemented bottles
for a fancy finish.

CLUSTERED BOTTLE VASE

Recycled items: four single-serving juice
bottles

You will also need white spray primer,
white spray paint, yellow and red acrylic
paint, paintbrushes, black permanent
fine-point marker, household cement, and
1¹/₂"w ribbon.

*Allow primer, paint, and household
cement to dry after each application.*

1. Apply primer to bottles. Spray paint
bottles white.
2. Paint red flowers on bottles. Paint
centers of flowers yellow. Use marker to
outline flowers.
3. For vase, use household cement to glue
bottles together.
4. Measure around vase; add 12". Cut
a length of ribbon the determined
measurement. Tie ribbon into a bow
around vase; notch ribbon ends.

HANDSOME HIDEAWAY

*M*ade from an ordinary shoe box, this handsome package can hide treasures and keepsakes. Spray paint the bottom of the box to set off the lid's "antique" finish, created using swirls of hot glue, aluminum foil, and paint.

FOIL SHOE BOX

Recycled item: shoe box

You will also need black spray paint, hot glue gun, heavy-duty aluminum foil, spray adhesive, craft knife, black acrylic paint, household sponge, paper towels, and clear acrylic spray sealer.

Refer to Painting Techniques, page 156, before beginning project.

1. Remove lid from box. Spray paint inside and outside of bottom of box black; allow to dry.
2. Use a pencil to draw swirls and dots on top and sides of lid. Use hot glue to draw over dots and swirls; allow to dry.
3. Cut a piece of foil large enough to cover top and sides of lid. Apply spray adhesive to top and sides of lid. Lightly crumple foil. Carefully uncrumple foil and press onto top and sides of lid. Use craft knife to trim foil even with edges of lid.

4. Working with one small area at a time, sponge paint foil on lid black. Use paper towels to wipe away excess paint; allow to dry.

5. Apply two to three coats of sealer to lid and bottom of box; allow to dry. Replace lid on box.

SUMMER MEMORIES

*I*t's easy to transform a greeting card box into a keeper for summer memories. This seaside extravaganza is decorated with seashells, fish netting, paint, and markers.

VACATION MEMORY BOX

Recycled item: greeting card box with a clear lid

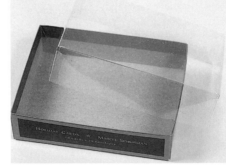

You will also need white, yellow, red, blue, and tan acrylic paint; paintbrushes; household sponges; craft glue; photograph; items to decorate inside of box (we used seashells and a scrap of fish netting); green paint pen; and a black permanent fine-point marker.

Refer to Painting Techniques, page 156, before beginning project. Allow paint and glue to dry after each application.

1. Remove lid from box. Paint inside of box blue and outside of box red. Sponge paint tan sand, white clouds, and a yellow sun on inside of box.
2. Arrange and glue photograph and decorative items in box. Place lid on box.
3. Sponge paint red border around edges of lid. Use paint pen to write "My Summer Memories!" on lid. Use marker to outline words.

"EGG-CELLENT" POSIES

*T*he *pretty posies on this
"egg-cellent" table topper are
actually made from foam egg
cartons! This unique decoration
is achieved by spray painting
foam cutouts, then gluing them
to a moss-covered topiary form.
Leaves, berries, and a bow add
the finishing touches.*

EGG CARTON TOPIARY

Recycled items: foam egg cartons

You will also need a low-temperature
glue gun, Design Master® green spray
paint, 6" dia. clay flowerpot, topiary form
to fit in a 6" dia. clay flowerpot, artificial
sheet moss, artificial leaves, artificial
berry picks, and 35" of 7/8"w sheer
ribbon.

1. For each flower, cut two cupped
sections from egg carton. Cut 3/8" from
bottom of one cupped section for flower
center. Glue cut edges of flower center to
inside of remaining cupped section. Trim
outer edges of flower to form petals.
2. Spray paint flowers and flowerpot
green; allow to dry.
3. Glue topiary form in flowerpot. Glue
moss in flowerpot to cover topiary form.
4. Glue moss, then flowers, leaves, and
berries to topiary balls. Tie ribbon into a
bow. Glue bow to top of topiary.

Cozy Sweater Wrap

Time to clean out your closet? Instead of throwing out your worn sweaters, recycle them to make a cozy afghan. We used an ensemble of white sweaters, but you can choose colorful variations to create a rainbow of snuggles.

SWEATER AFGHAN

Recycled items: four extra-large sweaters

Match right sides and raw edges and use a ¹/₄" seam allowance for all sewing. To prevent fraying, zigzag all raw edges.

1. Cut top portion from two sweaters, underarm to underarm (Fig. 1); discard top portions. Undo side seams to make four pieces. If necessary, trim pieces to same size.

Fig. 1

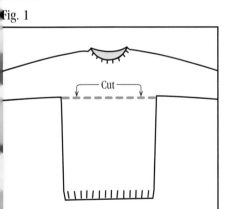

2. For each panel, matching waistband edges, place two pieces together. Sew along edges opposite waistband edges (Fig. 2). For afghan, matching long edges, sew panels together (Fig 3).

Fig. 2

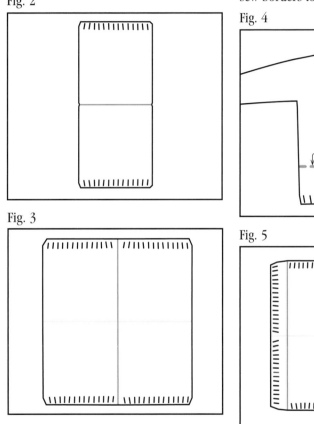

Fig. 3

3. For each border strip, measuring 8" from edge of waistband and cutting through all layers, cut one strip from each remaining sweater (Fig. 4). Undo one side seam. Trimming or stretching to fit, sew borders to afghan (Fig. 5).

Fig. 4

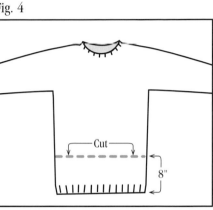

Fig. 5

CUSTOM-MADE ACCENT

*S*earching *for the perfect accent for your entryway? Start off on the right foot with a customized throw rug. It's easy and inexpensive using a carpet sample and acrylic paint! Not only will you finish fast, but you'll also have fun experimenting with patterns and colors!*

STENCILED CARPET SAMPLE

Recycled item: 18¹/₄" x 27¹/₂" light-color carpet sample

You will also need masking tape; pink, green, brown, and black acrylic paint; paintbrushes; stencil plastic; craft knife; cutting mat; and stencil brushes.

Allow paint to dry after each application.

1. Using masking tape to mask off each stripe, refer to Diagram to paint stripes on carpet.
2. Using Design A, Design B, and triangle patterns, page 147, follow *Stenciling*, page 157, to paint designs on carpet.

Diagram

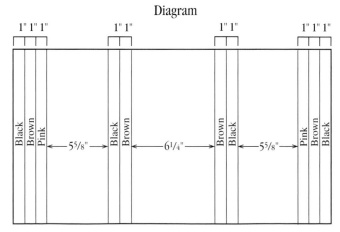

"ANTIQUE" LAP TRAY

*I*deal for snacking, reading, or catching up on correspondence, this antique-look lap tray really comes in handy! Decoupage a painted metal tray with old-fashioned paper motifs and then apply crackle medium for an aged look. Stuff coordinating fabric with packing peanuts to pad the bottom of the tray.

LAP TRAY

Recycled items: metal tray and foam packing peanuts

You will also need white spray primer, antique white spray paint, harvest-motif wrapping paper, craft glue, foam brush, crackle medium, glazing medium, antiquing stain, clear acrylic spray sealer, fabric, and a hot glue gun.

Allow primer, paint, crackle medium, glazing medium, and sealer to dry after each application.

1. Apply primer to tray. Spray paint tray.
2. Cut desired motifs from paper. Mix one part craft glue with one part water. Use foam brush to apply glue mixture to back of motifs. Arrange motifs on tray; smooth in place. Apply glue mixture over motifs; allow to dry.
3. Follow manufacturer's instructions to apply crackle medium to tray. Apply a thick coat of glazing medium over tray. Follow *Antiquing*, page 157, to apply stain to tray. Apply two to three coats of sealer to tray.
4. Draw around tray on wrong side of fabric. Cut out fabric 2" outside drawn line. Press raw edges of fabric 1/4" to wrong side. Leaving an opening for filling and gathering at corners as necessary, hot glue folded edge under lip of tray. Fill with packing peanuts. Hot glue opening closed.

PATTERNS

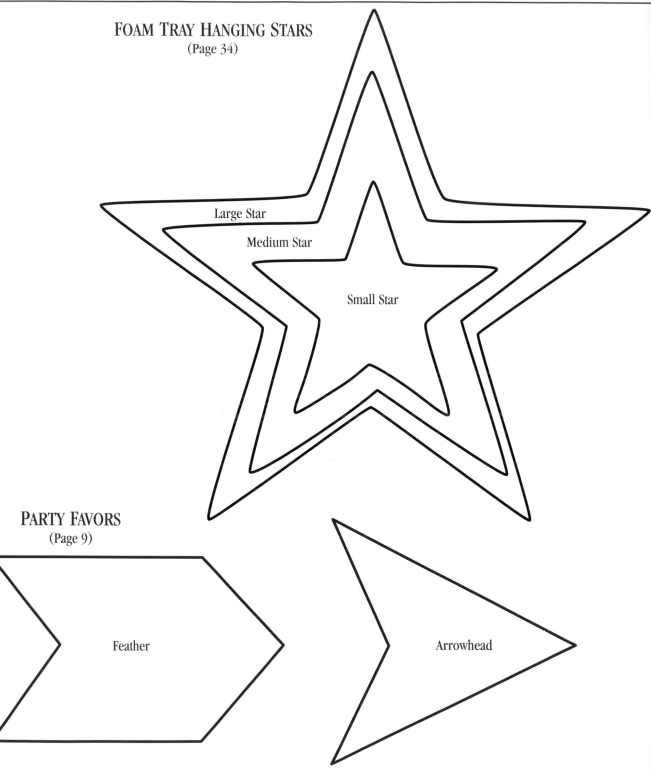

FOAM TRAY HANGING STARS
(Page 34)

Large Star

Medium Star

Small Star

PARTY FAVORS
(Page 9)

Feather

Arrowhead

"LETTER TO SANTA" HOLDER
(Page 31)

to: Santa
North Pole

From:

BIRDHOUSE CONDO
(Pages 71 and 72)

Star

Wing

Bird

Large
Heart

Small
Heart

Leisure Arts, Inc., grants permission to the
owner of this book to photocopy the label
design on this page for personal use only.

GARDEN SAMPLER
(Page 73)

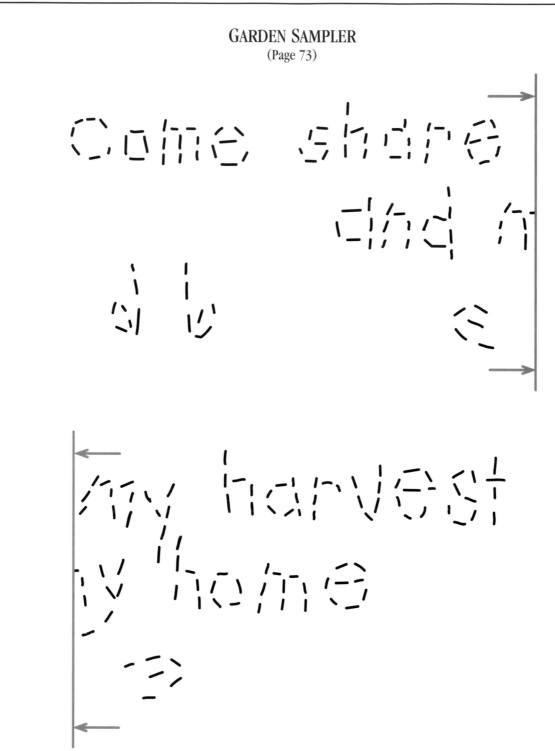

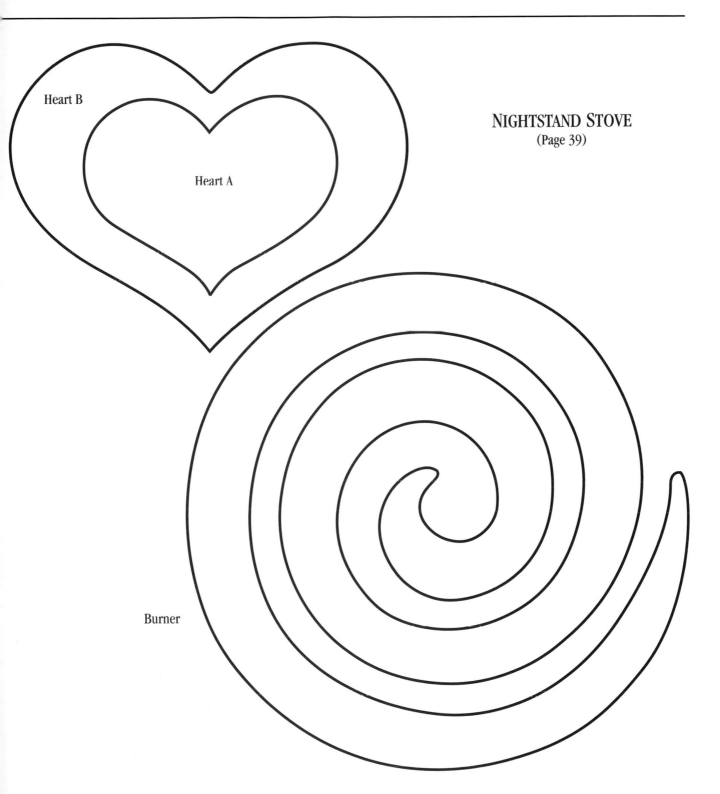

Heart B

Heart A

NIGHTSTAND STOVE
(Page 39)

Burner

COOKIE SHEET CLOWN
(Page 51)

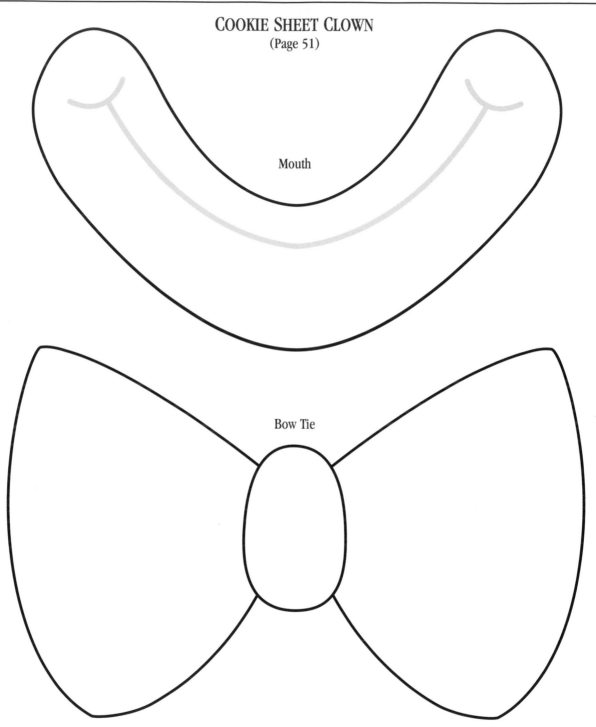

Mouth

Bow Tie

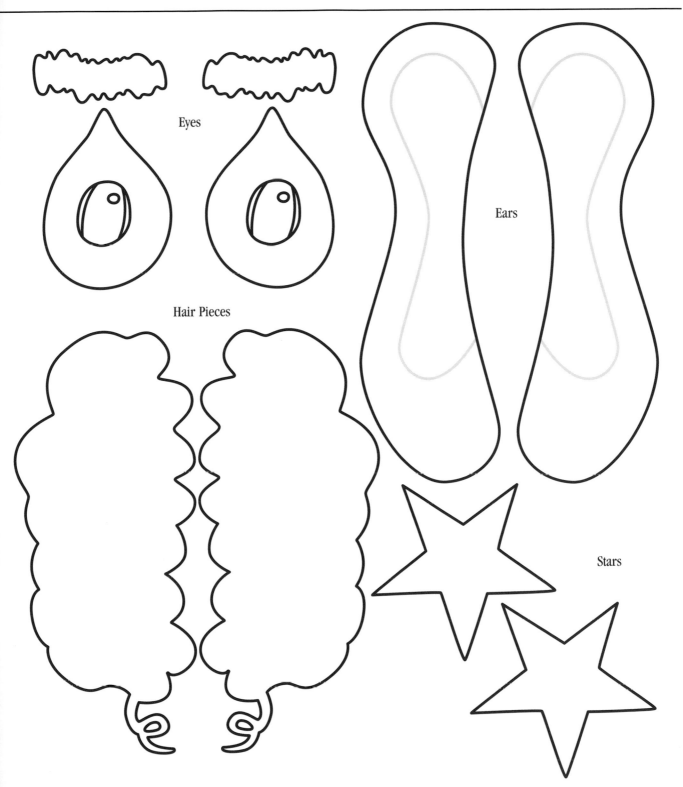

Eyes

Ears

Hair Pieces

Stars

SOCK CAT
(Page 43)

Ears

Heart

Nose

Muzzle

Eyes

Stripe

GLIDER
(Page 56)

STENCIL CUTTING KEY
Stencil #1
Stencil #2

COLOR KEY
Stencil #1 - white
Stencil #2 - green

Take Thyme
To Smell
The Flowers

PATRIOTIC BANNER
(Page 23)

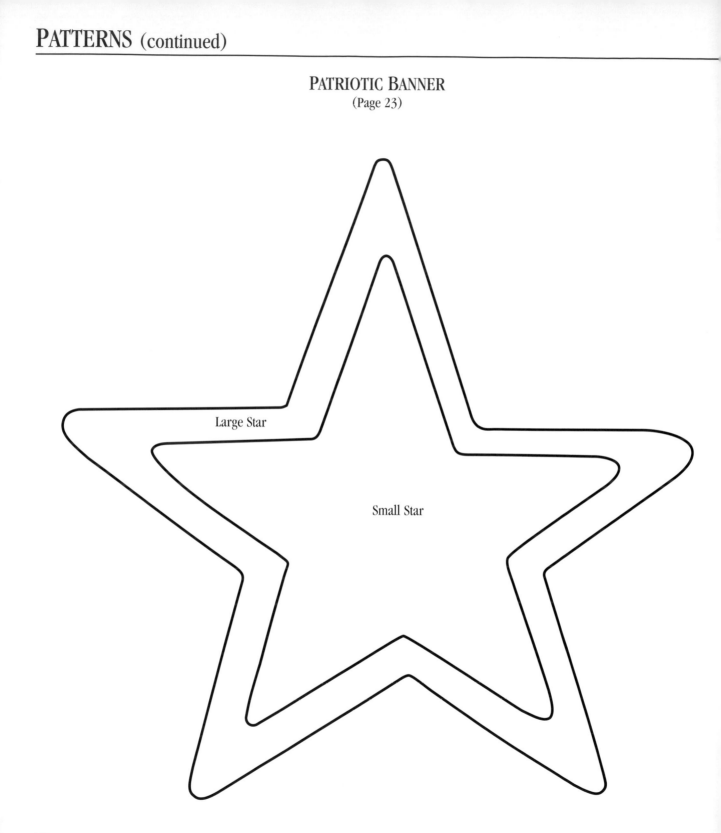

Large Star

Small Star

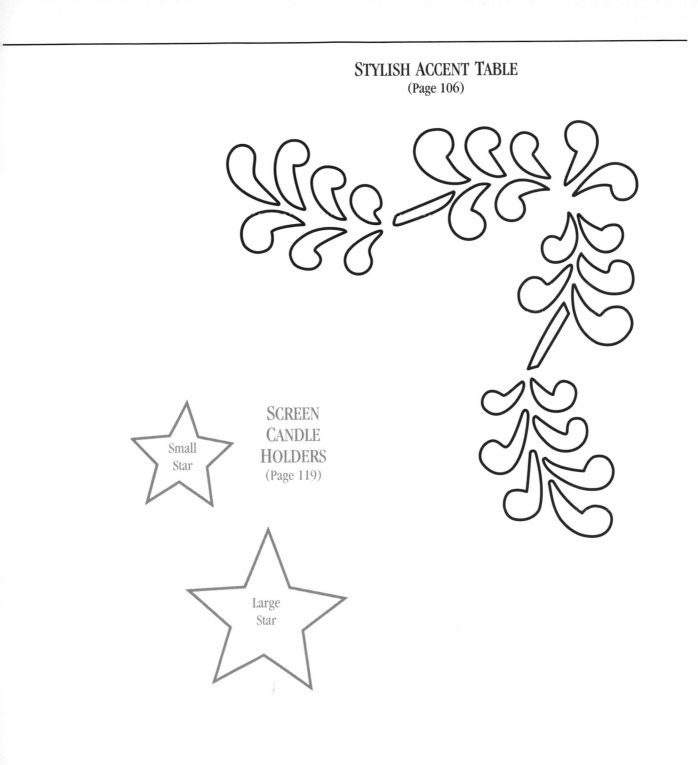

SCREEN
CANDLE
HOLDERS
(Page 119)

Small
Star

Large
Star

POSY PIGGY BANK
(Page 40)

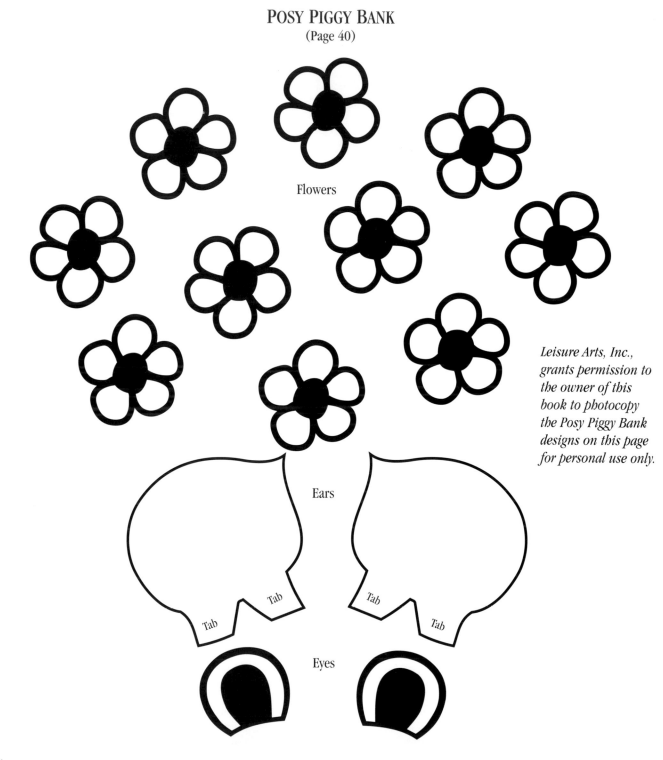

Flowers

Ears

Tab   Tab   Tab   Tab

Eyes

Leisure Arts, Inc., grants permission to the owner of this book to photocopy the Posy Piggy Bank designs on this page for personal use only.

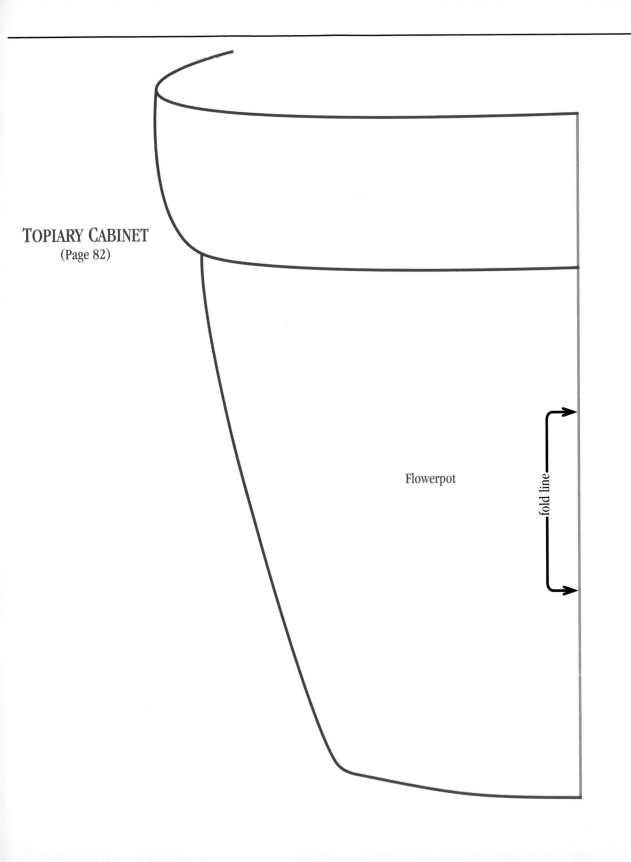

TOPIARY CABINET
(Page 82)

Flowerpot

fold line

YELLOW BUTTERFLY CHAIR
(Page 95)

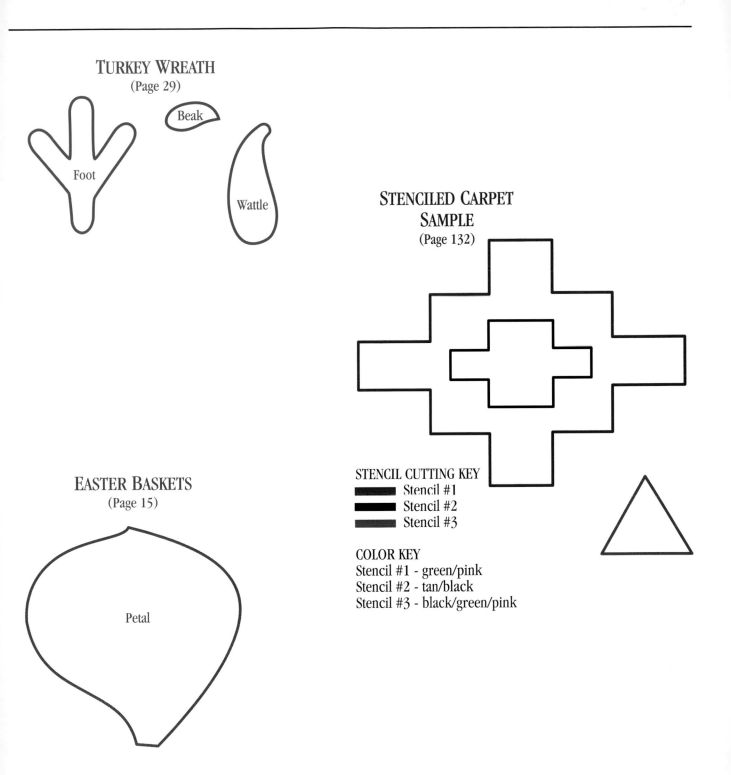

TURKEY WREATH
(Page 29)

Beak

Foot

Wattle

STENCILED CARPET SAMPLE
(Page 132)

STENCIL CUTTING KEY
Stencil #1
Stencil #2
Stencil #3

COLOR KEY
Stencil #1 - green/pink
Stencil #2 - tan/black
Stencil #3 - black/green/pink

EASTER BASKETS
(Page 15)

Petal

GARDENING JOURNAL
(Page 61)

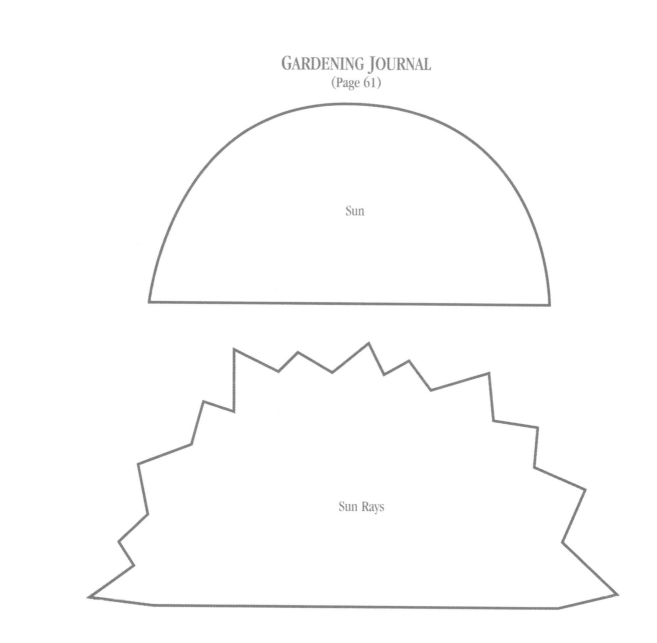

Sun

Sun Rays

WINDOWPANE FRAME
(Page 80)

Flower C

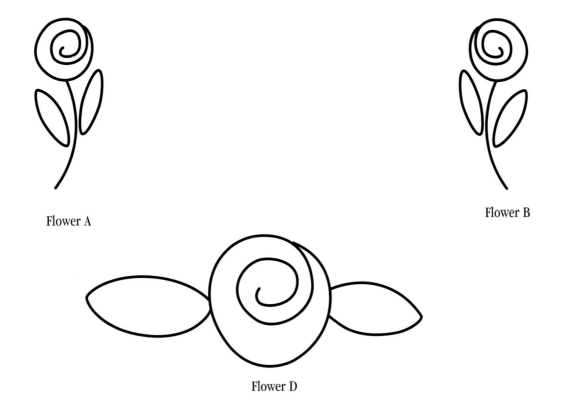

Flower A

Flower B

Flower D

GARDEN STAKES
(Page 63)

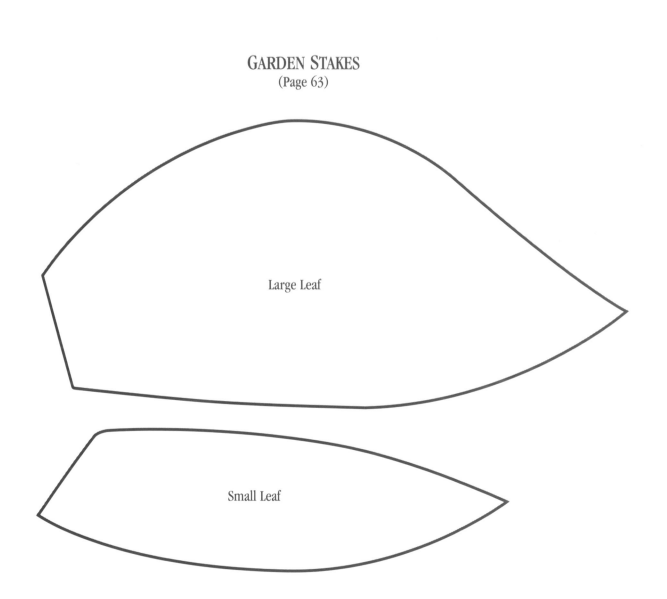

Large Leaf

Small Leaf

TEA TOWEL DOLL
(Page 123)

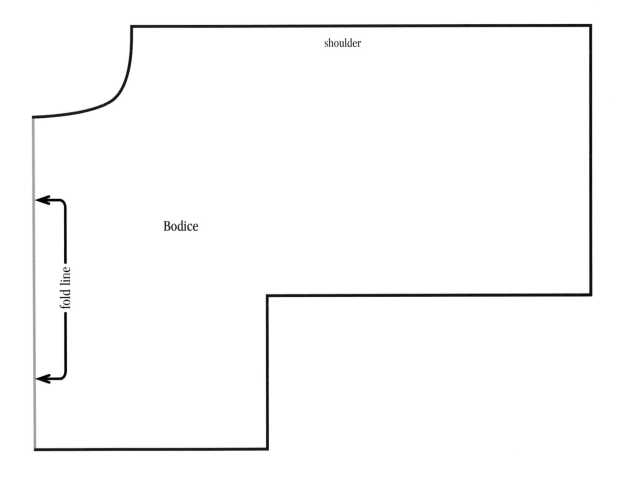

shoulder

Bodice

fold line

PATTERNS (continued)

CANISTERS AND PANS
(Page 41)

Heart A

Heart B

PLANTER
(Page 96)

STENCIL CUTTING KEY
Stencil #1
Stencil #2

COLOR KEY
Stencil #1 - pink
Stencil #2 - green

EASTER FLOOR MAT
(Page 13)

Egg

CRUSHED CAN FROGS
(Page 77)

Foot

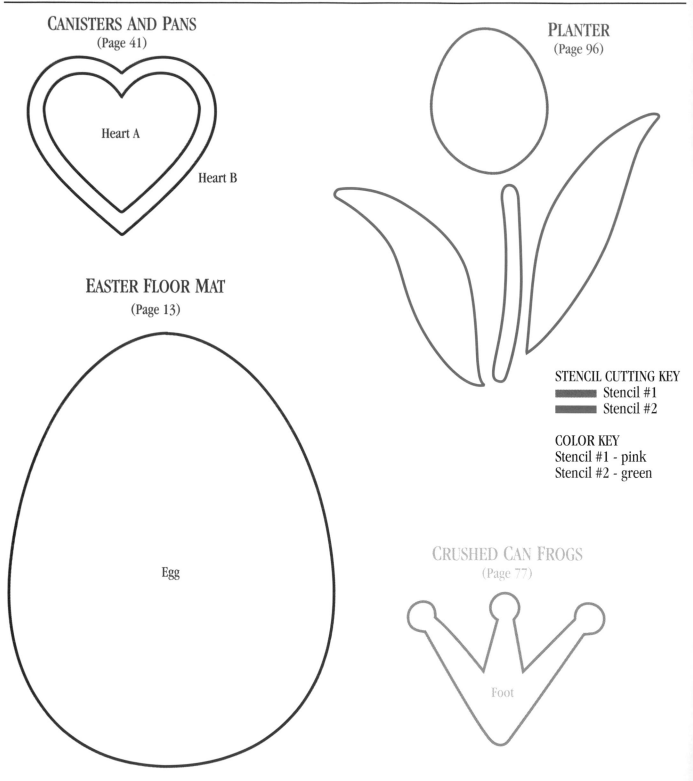

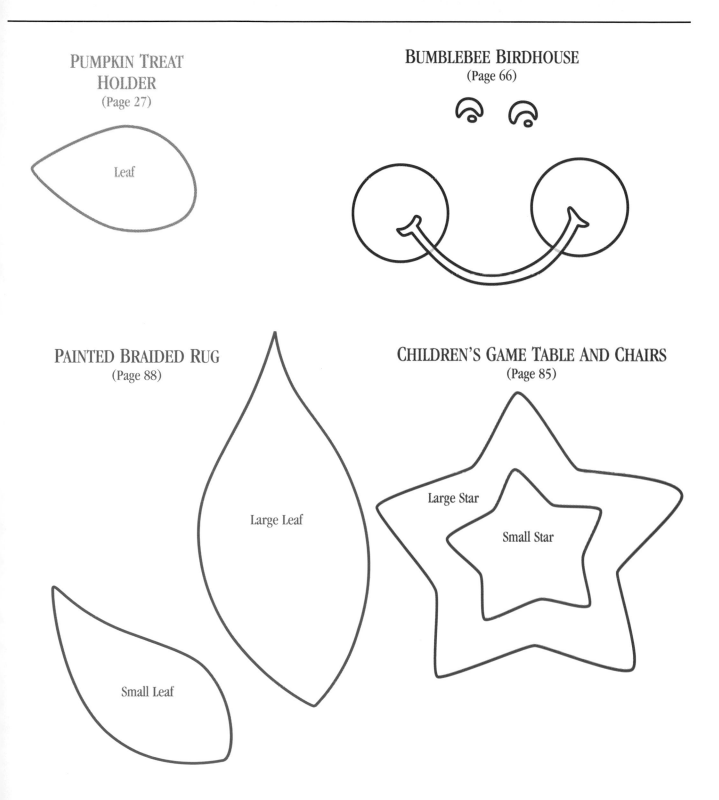

PUMPKIN TREAT HOLDER
(Page 27)

Leaf

BUMBLEBEE BIRDHOUSE
(Page 66)

PAINTED BRAIDED RUG
(Page 88)

Large Leaf

Small Leaf

CHILDREN'S GAME TABLE AND CHAIRS
(Page 85)

Large Star

Small Star

WINE BOTTLE CAROLERS
(Page 33)

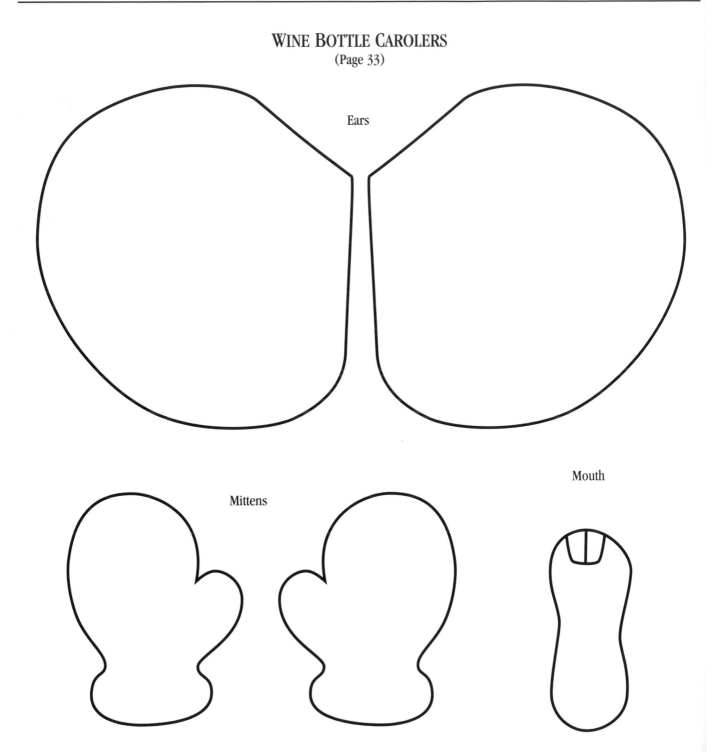

Ears

Mittens

Mouth

CRAYON HEADBOARD
(Page 48)

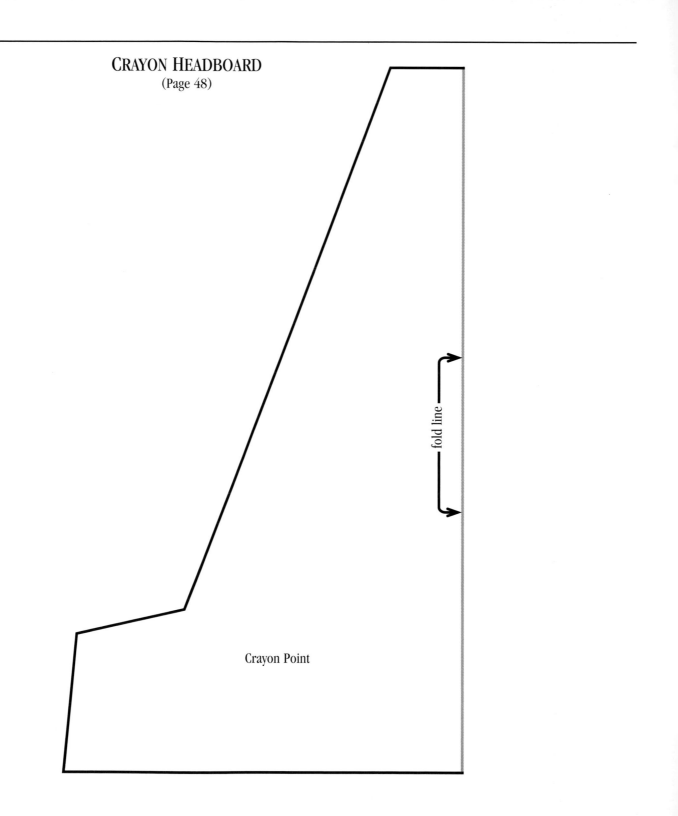

fold line

Crayon Point

GENERAL INSTRUCTIONS

ADHESIVES

When using any adhesive, carefully follow the manufacturer's instructions.

White craft glue: Recommended for paper. Dry flat.

Tacky craft glue: Recommended for paper, fabric, floral, or wood. Dry flat or secure items with clothespins or straight pins until glue is dry.

Craft glue stick: Recommended for paper or for gluing small, lightweight items to paper or other surface. Dry flat.

Fabric glue: Recommended for fabric or paper. Dry flat or secure items with clothespins or straight pins until glue is dry.

Decoupage glue: Recommended for decoupaging fabric or paper to a surface such as wood or glass. Use purchased decoupage glue or mix one part craft glue with one part water.

Hot or low-temperature glue gun: Recommended for paper, fabric, floral, or wood. Hold in place until set.

Rubber cement: Recommended for paper and cardboard. May discolor photos; may discolor paper with age. Dry flat (dries very quickly).

Spray adhesive: Recommended for paper or fabric. Can be repositionable or permanent. Dry flat.

Household cement: Recommended for ceramic or metal. Secure items with clothespins until glue is dry.

Wood glue: Recommended for wood. Nail, screw, or clamp items together until glue is dry.

COFFEE DYEING

1. Dissolve two tablespoons instant coffee in two cups hot water; allow to cool.
2. Soak fabric pieces in coffee several minutes. Remove from coffee. Allow to dry; press.

MAKING PATTERNS

For a more durable pattern, use a permanent pen to trace pattern onto stencil plastic.

WHOLE PATTERN

Place tracing paper over pattern and trace pattern; cut out.

HALF PATTERN
Indicated by blue line on pattern.

1. Fold tracing paper in half and match fold to blue line of pattern.
2. Trace pattern half; turn folded paper over and draw over traced lines on remaining side of paper.
3. Unfold paper and cut out pattern.

SECTIONED PATTERN
Indicated by grey line on pattern.

1. Trace one pattern section.
2. Matching grey lines and arrows, trace remaining section to complete pattern; cut out.

PREPARING AN ITEM FOR PAINTING

Caution: Work in a well-ventilated area when using cleaners. Wear protective gloves and clothing as needed. Cover work area with plastic or newspaper.

You will need household cleaner, sponge or scouring pad, and a soft damp cloth. *You may also need* fine-grit sandpaper or steel wool, tack cloth, and spray primer.

1. Use cleaner and sponge or scouring pad to clean item. Remove cleaner with damp cloth; allow to dry. If necessary, use fine-grit sandpaper or steel wool to remove rust. Wipe clean with tack cloth; allow to dry.
2. (*Note:* Unfinished metal items will need a coat of primer before applying base coat.) Follow project instructions to apply finishes.

PAINTING TECHNIQUES

TRANSFERRING A PATTERN
Trace pattern onto tracing paper. Place transfer paper coated side down between project and traced pattern. Use removable tape to secure pattern to project. Use a pencil to transfer outlines of design to project (press lightly to avoid smudges and heavy lines that are difficult to cover). If necessary, use a soft eraser to remove any smudges.

PAINTING BASE COATS

A disposable foam plate makes a good palette.

Use a medium round brush for large areas and a small round brush for small areas. Do not overload brush. Allowing to dry between coats, apply several thin coats of paint to project.

TRANSFERRING DETAILS

To transfer detail lines to design, reposition pattern and transfer paper over painted base coats and use a pencil to lightly transfer detail lines onto project.

ADDING DETAILS

Use a permanent pen to draw over detail lines.

DIMENSIONAL PAINT

Before painting on project, practice painting on scrap fabric or paper.

1. To keep paint flowing smoothly, turn bottle upside down and allow paint to fill tip of bottle before each use.
2. Clean tip often with a paper towel.
3. If tip becomes clogged, insert a straight pin into tip opening.
4. When painting lines or painting over appliqués, keep bottle tip in contact with surface of project, applying a line of paint centered over drawn line or raw edge of appliqué.
5. To correct a mistake, use a paring knife to gently scrape excess paint from project before it dries. Carefully remove stain with non-acetone nail polish remover. A mistake may also be camouflaged by incorporating the mistake into the design.
6. Lay project flat for 24 hours to ensure that paint has set.

SPONGE PAINTING

1. Dampen sponge with water.
2. Dip dampened sponge into paint; blot on paper towel to remove excess paint.
3. Use a light stamping motion to paint project.

SPATTER PAINTING

1. Place item on flat surface.
2. Mix one part paint with one part water. Dip toothbrush in diluted paint and pull thumb firmly across bristles to spatter paint on item. Repeat until desired effect is achieved. Allow to dry.

ANTIQUING

"Antiquing" can be applied to bare wood, over paint, or over a clear finish. Test this technique on an inconspicuous area of the item you are antiquing to ensure desired results.

For stain, use brown waterbase stain or mix one part brown acrylic paint with one part water. Working on one small area at a time, use foam brush to apply stain to item; blot or wipe immediately with a soft cloth to remove excess stain. Allow to dry. Repeat as desired for darker antiquing.

WEATHERED WHITEWASH TECHNIQUE

Allow paint and wax to dry between applications and before sanding.

Use fine-grit sandpaper to smooth rough areas on wood; remove dust with tack cloth. Apply base coat to wood according to project instructions. For "worn" areas on finished piece, randomly apply paste floor wax to wood. Use white acrylic paint to paint wood. Use sandpaper to remove paint over waxed areas.

STENCILING

These instructions are written for multicolor stencils. For single-color stencils, make one stencil for entire design.

1. For first stencil, cut a piece from stencil plastic 1" larger than entire pattern. Center plastic over pattern and use a permanent pen to trace outlines of all areas of first color in stencil cutting key. For placement guidelines, outline remaining colored areas using dashed lines. Using a new piece of plastic for each additional color in stencil cutting key, repeat for remaining stencils.
2. Place each plastic piece on cutting mat and use craft knife to cut out stencil along solid lines, making sure edges are smooth.
3. Hold or tape stencil in place. Using a clean, dry stencil brush or sponge piece, dip brush or sponge in paint. Remove excess paint on a paper towel. Brush or sponge should be almost dry to produce best results. Beginning at edge of cutout area, apply paint in a stamping motion over stencil. If desired, highlight or shade design by stamping a lighter or darker shade of paint in cutout area. Repeat until all areas of first stencil have been painted. Carefully remove stencil and allow paint to dry.
4. Using stencils in order indicated in color key and matching guidelines on stencils to previously stenciled areas, repeat Step 3 for remaining stencils.

GENERAL INSTRUCTIONS (continued)

EMBROIDERY STITCHES

FRENCH KNOT
Bring needle up at 1. Wrap floss once around needle and insert needle at 2, holding floss with non-stitching fingers (Fig. 1). Tighten knot as close to fabric as possible while pulling needle back through fabric. For larger knot, use more strands of floss; wrap only once.

Fig. 1

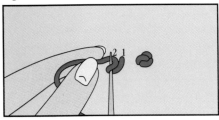

RUNNING STITCH
Make a series of straight stitches with stitch length equal to the space between stitches (Fig. 2).

Fig. 2

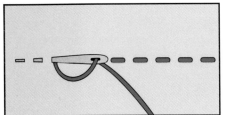

MAKING A RUCHED FLOWER

Ribbon length is given in project instructions.

1. Beginning 1" from left end, mark top edge of ribbon at 2" intervals. Beginning 2" from left end, mark bottom edge of ribbon at 2" intervals. Lightly mark a diagonal line between top and bottom edges where marked (Fig. 1).

Fig. 1

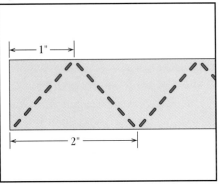

2. Using a double strand of matching thread, and knotting at one end, work a *Running Stitch* along drawn lines, pulling thread while stitching to gather.
3. To form flower, coil ribbon into a circle, tacking as necessary.

COVERING A LAMPSHADE

1. To make pattern, find seamline of lampshade. If shade does not have a seamline, draw a vertical line from top edge to bottom edge of shade.
2. Centering tissue paper edge on shade seamline, tape in place. Wrap paper around shade extending one inch past seamline; tape to secure (Fig. 1).

Fig. 1

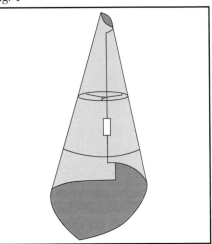

3. Trace along top and bottom edges of shade. Draw a vertical line from top edge to bottom edge of shade 1" past seamline. Remove paper; cut along drawn lines.
4. Use pattern to cut cover from desired fabric or paper.
5. Fold one straight edge of covering $1/2$" to wrong side; press.
6. Matching unpressed straight edge of covering to seamline, use spray adhesive to apply covering to shade. Use glue to secure pressed edge.

ADDING WELTING

1. Matching raw edges and beginning and ending 3" from ends of welting, glue welting to project. To make turning corners easier, clip seam allowance of welting at corners.

2. Remove approximately 3" of seam at one end of welting; fold fabric away from cord. Trim remaining end of welting so that cord ends meet exactly (Fig. 1).

Fig. 1

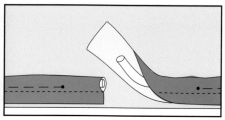

3. Fold short edge of welting fabric ½" to wrong side; fold fabric back over area where ends meet (Fig. 2).

Fig. 2

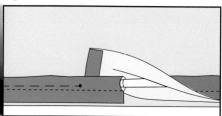

4. Glue remainder of welting to project along edges.

MAKING A FABRIC YO-YO

1. Use compass to draw a circle on tracing paper the diameter indicated in project instructions. Use pattern to cut out fabric circle.

2. Turn raw edge of circle ¼" to wrong side.

3. Using a double strand of thread, work a small *Running Stitch*, page 158, along turned edge.

4. Pull ends of thread to tightly gather circle; knot thread.

5. Flatten circle with gathers at center.

COVERING A BOX

1. Cut a piece of paper large enough to cover box. Center box on wrong side of paper and draw around box.

2. Use ruler to draw lines ½" outside drawn lines, extending lines to edges of paper. Draw diagonal lines from intersections of outer lines to corners of original lines.

3. Cut away corners of paper and clip along diagonal lines (Fig. 1).

Fig. 1

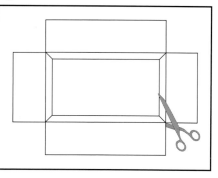

4. Apply spray adhesive to wrong side of paper.

5. Center box on paper, matching box to original drawn lines; smooth paper on bottom of box.

6. To cover front and back of box, smooth paper onto front and back sides of box. Smooth excess paper around corners onto adjacent sides. Smooth paper to inside of box, clipping as necessary (Fig. 2).

Fig. 2

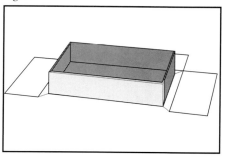

7. To cover each end, smooth paper onto end of box. Use craft knife and ruler to trim excess paper even with corners. Smooth paper to inside of box.

CREDITS

We want to extend a warm *thank you* to the generous people who allowed us to photograph our projects at their homes: Nancy Appleton, Terry Dilday, Virginia Hickingbotham, Joe and Ellison Madden, Duncan and Nancy Porter, John and Jane Prather, Leighton Weeks, and Nancy Zuerlein.

To Wisconsin Technicolor LLC of Pewaukee, Wisconsin, we say thank you for the superb color reproduction and excellent pre-press preparation.

We especially want to thank photographers Mark Mathews, Larry Pennington, Karen Shirey, and Ken West of Peerless Photography, and Jerry R. Davis of Jerry Davis Photography, all of Little Rock, Arkansas, for their time, patience, and excellent work.

We extend a special word of thanks to Kelly Hepner, who designed the *Stenciled Carpet Sample* on page 132.